The Green Lane
to Nowhere

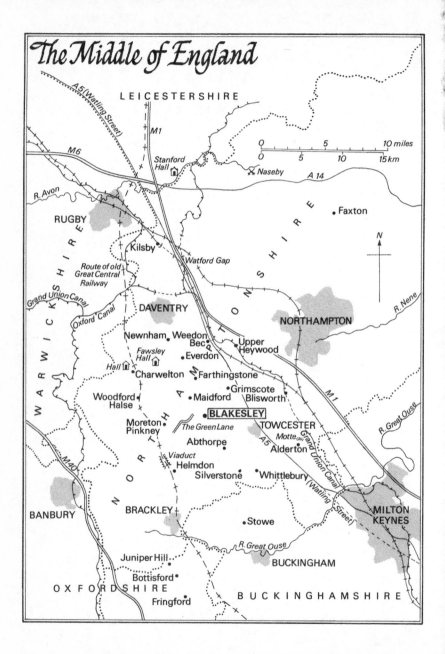

The Middle of England

LEICESTERSHIRE

A5 (Watling Street)

M1

M6

Stanford Hall

R. Avon

Naseby

A 14

RUGBY

Faxton

Kilsby

Watford Gap

N

R. Nene

WARWICKSHIRE

Route of old Great Central Railway

Grand Union Canal

Oxford Canal

DAVENTRY

NORTHAMPTONSHIRE

NORTHAMPTON

Newnham

Weedon Bec

Upper Heywood

Fawsley Hall

Hall

Everdon

Charwelton

Farthingstone

Woodford Halse

Maidford

Grimscote

Blisworth

Moreton Pinkney

The Green Lane

BLAKESLEY

TOWCESTER

Motte

M1

R. Great Ouse

Abthorpe

Alderton

A5

Grand Union Canal (Watling Street)

M40

Viaduct

Helmdon

Silverstone

Whittlebury

BRACKLEY

MILTON KEYNES

BANBURY

Stowe

Juniper Hill

R. Great Ouse

BUCKINGHAM

Bottisford

OXFORDSHIRE

Fringford

BUCKINGHAMSHIRE

0   5   10 miles

0   5   10   15 km

The Sunday Telegraph

Byron Rogers

THE GREEN LANE TO NOWHERE

The Life of an English Village

AURUM PRESS

First published in Great Britain
2002 by Aurum Press Ltd
25 Bedford Avenue, London WC1B 3AT

These pieces appeared in earlier form in the
Sunday Telegraph, *Sunday Express*,
Evening Standard and *Country Living* and *Saga* magazines.

A catalogue record for this book is available from the British Library.

ISBN 1 85410 785 2

1 3 5 7 9 10 8 6 4 2
2002   2004   2006   2005   2003

Set in 11 on 12.75pt Perpetua by M Rules
Designed by Peter Ward
Map by Reg Piggott

Printed in Great Britain by MPG Books Ltd, Bodmin

To George Freeston of Blisworth

CONTENTS

CONTENTS

BEGINNINGS

WE CAME IN A DEAD TIME, moving the furniture in on the first day of the New Year. Around 3 p.m. we had finished, for we had little enough to move, and were driving away when, just outside the village, we saw two parrots. Whoppers, the size of small turkeys, they were flying slowly and steadily towards the west as though they knew exactly where they were going, and if my wife hadn't seen them as well, I should have joined BUPA that week, for against a bleak January landscape it was as though some huge child had managed to open a paint-box: the reds and blues exploded in that sky.

Much later it was a great joke in the village. 'Crows,' said Albert; each time we met he would ask after my friends, 'them parrats'. But after that, few things surprised us about the English countryside in the late twentieth century, and certainly not the nostalgia for it, which was abruptly everywhere. That summer a new glossy magazine appeared, aimed at no specific age group or sports enthusiasts, but 'at people who live in the country *and those who aspire to do so*'. The italics are mine, but the latter seemed to be the more important. In its beginnings *Country Living* was based on the commercial premise that there were enough potential readers who believed that life there was somehow superior.

The Countryside Commission announced that 84 per cent of the population visited the country for recreation, so looking in on rural England had become the most popular national leisure activity. You came on men who had about as much contact with the country as they had with the KGB, talking about their heritage. Farmers, they said bitterly in saloon bars, were trustees for the rest of us.

But what they and the Commission had forgotten was that the overwhelming majority of that 84 per cent was descended from people who were once on the run from rural England. In 1850 for the first time in the recorded history of all the nations of the earth, more people lived in the towns and cities of Britain than in the countryside, having left this for the reasons men had always left the land – for jobs, money, excitement, freedom. Earlier they had fled it to escape feudalism, flight and death being the only means of escape, though just three miles from where I am writing this, in what must be the most extraordinary law case of the Middle Ages, a man tried another way. Stephen of Adstone took his feudal overlord, the abbot of Canons Ashby, to court to establish that he was a free man. He lost, but he must have moved heaven and earth to get that far.

Those who write so movingly about disappearing hedges forget that in the classic of country life, *Lark Rise to Candleford*, hedges hung like doom over that small hamlet. Flora Thompson has her old people talk of a Golden Age when they still had their ancient rights to commonland, rights which went when the hedges came. They had not forgotten their sense of betrayal. On a tombstone in Hampshire these words were cut: 'England made her choice long ago / Wealth. Cities, industry / All countrymen know.'

Then in the 1970s two things happened. In a time of inflation, accountants and the men who administered pension funds had a vision of woods and green places. The land had always been the safest investment (and the best way of laundering dubious money) but what was new was the scale of purchase, with £2000 an acre commonplace; farmers were paper millionaires overnight.

For the rest there was nostalgia. It was in reaction against the changes they saw taking place around them in the cities, their worries about crime and education, that people began thinking wistfully of a traditional world and one on a more human scale. They remembered fields full of folk they had once seen from cars, and the small, untidy mixed farms of their childhood: the rusting cars, the puppies playing in the barns, places where, they assumed, nothing had changed. Those who could, sought their dream (a strange little fact that went largely unnoticed was that in the 1981 census the population of London fell for the first time since 1901).

And I should know. It was for such reasons, not for any job, that I moved to the country. I had been away just thirty-five years. I was born in the countryside near Carmarthen, from where my parents moved to the town, and to the English language, which, at five, I was unable to speak. Before that my people, farmers and agricultural labourers, streaming away until beyond three generations they were lost in a haze of rural poverty, had had no choice in the matter. Change came quickly: of my twenty-one cousins, only one is now a Welsh farmer. Yet here I was, going back, following a dream compounded partly of my own childhood and partly of old film comedies where Margaret Rutherford is forever the district nurse and Bernard Miles behind the bar, parts they probably never played, and there are flagged floors and fires and gleaming brass (the perfect pub was an essential part of the dream). It was as barmy as that.

But following it meant that for three years I drew circles on maps, mooched around small towns, met young men whom the multinationals were twitching away, sad wives whose husbands had disappeared, and world-weary teenagers whose parents were breaking up. You get to see a lot of misery when you look for houses in the country.

You can also come a cropper. It was an Oxfordshire cottage with honeysuckle climbing the walls, and was beautiful, though it did have one drawback: the ceilings were so low I couldn't stand up in the house. No trouble, said the woman brightly: you had only to lower the floors, and I, who had spent the lunch-hour in the idyllic local, nodded. It was a stone floor, the flags lying as they had lain for 200 years; we would have needed gelignite.

But that was nothing on Rose Cottage. Blackcurrants and a beech tree and the garden heavy with summer. There was also a well out of a nursery rhyme, a round bricked well with a bucket clanking in darkness, the rope moving easily – but it moved easily for one reason. The well was *used*. The house was not on the mains or on the National Grid or on any sewerage system. A building society would as soon have advanced money on a yurt in Middle England as on Rose Cottage. Yet I bid at auction for it and was much put out when it went for £27,000. I have often wondered since about the man who bought it, a dreamer even further down the path of the Great Return.

In the end we bought a house in that odd lost triangle of land where Oxfordshire, Warwickshire and Northamptonshire meet, which the main roads circle and to which few tourists come. There were small hiccups at the start, the building society surveyor finding a bulge in the cellar wall; but then it was, he reported gloomily, an old house, and old houses moved. Eventually the money came through, and we came, my wife and I, on 1 January 1980.

We knew nothing about the village to which we had come; we knew no one. Like most people moving into the countryside in the late twentieth century, we had for all practical purposes materialised like travellers in space and time. A city is a small place, you mix with your own kind and make your own world there, so time starts with your coming. But a village is a large place, it has a past. Events, traditions and economic circumstances exist that have shaped it and the inhabitants you now meet.

So you have a choice. Either you regard the place in which you find yourself as a film set, 'a view' as my holidaying sisters-in-law say, into which weekly you unpack your Waitrose plastic bags, or you try to graft yourself onto the experiences of, in my case, George Freeston, John Butler, Ray Reynolds and others, Northamptonshire men, remembrancers all. That way doors open in the landscape, on drama, mystery, and, yes, on change. For I did find change. I did not expect to but I did. This is what gives this book its structure, its setting a composite of some four villages almost exactly in the middle of England. In it, in these collected articles and columns, you may get a glimpse of what life was like in the English countryside at the turn of the twenty-first century.

I have lived here twenty-two years, in this village and this house. My daughter was born here, who now, aged nineteen and a university student, cannot wait to get away to the towns. Another cycle starts, just as this book starts, in time.

Byron Rogers, Blakesley, 2002

PART ONE

APPROACHES
IN TIME

The Village

THE VILLAGE LIES in a pleat of Middle England like a toy lost in a counterpane. 'Shouldn't bother about house insurance,' said my friend the probation officer. 'It's enough of a strain on the IQ just finding the bloody place.' No church tower on the skyline, no main roads; this is something you stumble on. And it had to be once, with the Danelaw starting just four miles away at Watling Street. When the immigrants in the horned hats got tired of farming or trading or whatever it was they did when the tracks were too bad for long-range massacre, they were obliged to prey on their neighbours. This was a war zone.

Still, the young managed to find their way out, like the poet Dryden, to London, to 'torture one poor word ten-thousand ways'. It is odd to think, looking from my window, that the rental of those fields made lines like that possible. The village was the one thing Dryden inherited from his father, and it was worth £60 a year to him.

But mostly it was a place where strangers turned up. I have a Victorian gazetteer in front of me and, among the farmers, maltsters, butchers and blacksmiths, is this: 'James Hutchins, artist'. Where had he come from in 1849? Or, in 1416, the chap with the Zapata moustache in plate armour, entombed behind the font, Matthew Swettenham, 'Bearer of the Bow' to Henry IV?

Nobody knows what duties that involved, for the title is mentioned nowhere else in English history. Not an archer definitely, for the tomb is too grand for a man on fourpence a day plus expenses, which was then the going rate for the French wars. It is also not known what Swettenham was doing in the village, for he is mentioned in history as one of Richard II's New Men whose promotion prompted such envy. Most of these perished with the king, but clearly not Swettenham. Like Richard's roan ('that jade hath eat bread from my Royal hand'), he made some deal with the usurper and so lies here in brass.

He probably would not have gone to London much in his last years, not with the skulls of his old mates gleaming on London Bridge; he stayed here, enjoying his mysterious quango and twitching whenever servants brought news of a stranger in the village, a bit like Billy Bones in *Treasure Island*. I see in the church visitors book (just seven pages filled in ten years) that in 1981 two Swettenhams came but left no comments.

The past has this way of stopping you suddenly here, like a tree root in a flowerbed. Walk through the fields at sunset and you see the ridges and furrows of the old ploughs rising in the shadow. Stand in the over-filled graveyard and peer over the wall at the trefoils in a window, all that remains of the Priory. The man who bought that in my time was one of two friends who both had lorries when the gold rush came, which other men called the M1. They drove them there and one broke down the first day, but not the lorry belonging to this man. Twenty years later he came to the village to hustle the house back to its medieval origins, regardless of expense.

A whole floor went, great beams were revealed (or quietly supplied) and a minstrels' gallery conjured out of air. I watched entranced from my window as a lawn came and, even more entranced, as it sank the next day. But then children were born and their father was obliged to move out, leaving the largest two-bedroomed house in England to baffle the estate agents.

They love this village ('a much sought-after place') and must writhe at the sight of the windmill which is falling apart. One man used to climb that regularly, for the sunsets, he claimed, until it was found he was photographing nude bathing parties. Charlie keeps his fleet of elderly tractors at the windmill's foot. A retired engineer, Charlie has no land, just tractors, which he exhibits at village fêtes. He was on the loudspeaker once, talking crankshafts, when the Americans sent an F1-11 over at 200 feet.

Curious lot, the American military. It was their attempt at local PR after the Libyan bombing raid. They forgot that at that height you are made to feel part of the Book of Revelations. The overwhelming black bulk of the Battlestar Galactica scraped by over the marmalade and the hoop-las, but Charlie did not look up or even pause in the commentary. It was his finest hour.

1989, 1990

Sunset on Watling Street

THIS WILL NOT take long. But then, that is the only thing which interests us about a road, the time it takes us to go from A to B, and at most it takes a quarter of an hour to drive along the A5 from Towcester in Northamptonshire to the Watford Gap service station. A quarter of an hour and 2000 years. For this is the old road, this is Watling Street.

Those ten miles we are travelling will not be so familiar to your children as they were once to you, for there is another road now, a few miles to the east, but all it takes is some incident on the M1, a pile-up, a widening of the carriageways, for there to be a return to the old road. It has happened to you, it will again, so what follows may reconcile you to those ten congested miles.

Listen, they are coming, the men who built Watling Street, and it is a terrible sound, the unhurried crunch of 6000 pairs of hob-nailed soles in step on paving stones. 'A long, slow stride that never varies from sunrise to sunset . . . Twenty four miles in eight hours, neither more nor less. Head and spear up, shield on your back, *cuirass* collar open one hand's breadth – and that's how you take the Eagles through Britain,' wrote Kipling in *Puck of Pook's Hill*. When the Roman Army invaded in the middle of the first century AD, it just walked across Britain. Consider this: when the Romans attacked Maiden Castle in Dorset, the strongest hill fort of all, they walked in. There is no archaeological evidence of siege works of any kind.

Six thousand men to a legion. Enlistment for twenty years. Fifty pounds of kit on every man's back. Porridge and bread. The walking walls of Rome and the terrible, steady sound of feet on the roads they themselves had built. Dover to London to St Albans to Dunstable to Towcester, and then north-west to Wroxeter and Shrewsbury: the foundations of the A5 which you drive along were laid by these men. Five layers. The hard earth foundation, the bed of stones, the layer of small stones mixed with mortar, then a layer of lime, gravel, pounded brick and tiles, whatever was to hand, and then the paved surface. At first this would have been a walking road, some 20 feet across, and then, as trade and traffic built up, it would have been doubled in size.

A moment of national emergency. Boudicca's rising had left Colchester, St Albans and London in ruin, their inhabitants massacred, when down that road came the 14th and 20th legions, still with that step, until somewhere south of where we are now there was the last battle.

The small towns along the road had their origins as service stations which became trading posts which became towns, a fate which would have been that of the motorway service stations in our time had not legislation forbidden this. See the pubs in Towcester? It is possible there were pubs on those sites in Roman times. See the church? In 1938 the vicar, trying to recover the lost church silver, dug near the porch and saw the earth begin to fall into the hole. He found himself staring at the remains of a central heating system bigger and more efficient than anything his church would ever know. It is thought this might have been a bath-house for the travellers passing through.

The hardest thing to grasp about the road you are travelling on is that it was once part of a world as organised as ours, which has completely disappeared. The lorries pound through Towcester at night now, just as the carts creaked through almost 2000 years ago, a law of the second century having closed the streets of Roman towns to commercial traffic during the hours of daylight.

Inns at 20- to 30-mile intervals, post-houses at 10-mile intervals offering the change of horses which allowed Imperial couriers to ride 50 miles in a day. A post house might have been the origin for the one great mysterious bend in the road north of Towcester at Whilton. It may even have puzzled you, just as it puzzled men for hundreds of years, until in the eighteenth century they recognised under the fields the 30 buried acres of Bannaventa, one town along the road which did not survive.

Towcester itself was a place of ruin for two centuries or more, but men still used Watling Street. We know this because alongside it there turned up one of the treasures of Saxon England, a sixth-century gold and silver belt stud set with jewels, dropped by some passing grandee.

But by the late ninth, early tenth century, the road is the most important road in England, with armies of probably no more than a few hundred men bustling up it. It is a frontier between Denmark and England, the Danes on one side of Watling Street, the English on the other. Think of that for a moment. The road you are on was an international frontier and a war zone.

The amazing thing is that the road survives and is still useable in Norman times, a thousand years and more after the sound of feet in step was last heard on this island. It is not known who repaired it in the Middle Ages, but probably, as elsewhere, this was the work of some religious house, but they did it well enough for Richard II to have been able to gallop 80 miles along it one night, from Daventry to London, to cope with some crisis in his crisis-ridden reign.

Eighty miles in a single night, and just over 200 years later, in November 1605, the one known record of the Middle Ages is about to be broken. On 5 November 1605 to be exact. Are you with me? For weeks a Mr Ambrose Rookwood, a young Catholic gentleman, has been arranging for relays of horses to be ready at the post houses of St Albans, Dunstable, Towcester and Daventry, and it is the gossip of the day. It is a terrible night of wind and rain when the riders come, riding not for the record but for their lives. The Gunpowder Plot has been discovered, and Rookwood and his fellow conspirators, Robert Catesby among them, are riding through the night to the latter's house at Ashby St Ledgers, one and a half miles from the Watford Gap service station. They cover the 80 miles up Watling Street in seven hours, but it is of no use. Death awaits them all.

The road they rode on is the one you are driving along. You can still see the house they made for; in fact, it could be yours, for it has been up for sale at a couple of million pounds for the last few years.

Then, after 1500 years, the road enters its second Golden Age: it is the late eighteenth century and the coaches have come. Look at the town of Towcester as it still is. All those grand buildings, with the wide arches cut into them, come from a time when twenty coaches stopped in twenty-four hours, and it is a time of records again, for the great engineer Telford has been loosed on Watling Street. It is the Holyhead Road now, 260 miles of resurfaced material, for the paving stones have gone underground and the ruts filled. The gradients have gone too; for it was said of Telford's road that no horse was reduced to walking pace unless he particularly wished it at any point between Holyhead and London.

As a result, the Holyhead Mail clocked a staggering 10½ miles an hour, not once or twice, *but throughout the entire journey* – and that included stoppages. This was faster than anything else on the roads of England; not even the Quicksilver covering the 175 miles from London to Exeter in eighteen hours, at an average speed of 9.72 mph, came close.

In the 1830s the competition was with the railways until these swept all before them, and even the Irish Mail was switched to the permanent way, which was not only faster, but much, much cheaper. There is a cruel irony in the fact that on the road you are travelling you can still see the competition, the main railway line to the north-west and the Grand Union canal being within 100 yards of each other, and with Watling Street, at Weedon.

And as the road went into decline, so did the little towns that depended on it. Towcester, which had been a bigger service station than anything on the motorways now, did not die as Roman Towcester had died; it became a moment of frozen Georgian grandeur. The inns were there, and the courtyards; it was just that the coaches no longer called. There was a railway station, but that did not count, for the line was a branch line.

The oldest inhabitant told me this story. 'We used to have this horse, pulled a cab between the Saracen's Head and the station. Won the Grand National in 1906. Rubio, his name was.'

'You mean, he won it before he pulled the cab?'

'No, no. During. Sixty-to-one, he was. Pulling the cab one week, winning the National the next, then back in harness again.'

'Good God.'

The town was rescued by the road when that in turn filled up again with people. The petrol engine had come to Watling Street but the petrol engine was a Sorcerer's Apprentice by the latter half of the twentieth century, with traffic pounding through the little towns. And it was now that the strangest development came on Watling Street: the Watford Gap service station opened on the M1 just a quarter of a mile from the old road. It was strange because you were forbidden to enter this from the countryside and forbidden to leave it. The world was streaming by again, just as it had on the railway, and this time the old road began to dwindle.

If you drive north, beyond that 10-mile section, you will find, when new dual carriageways have been built, that Watling Street at Tamworth has even lost its status as an A-road, being called the B-something or other, though it has not lost its older name. It is still Watling Street. But there can be no more rescues now; you are seeing the old road in its final sunset.

1996

The Charter

WE ARE ABOUT to go for a walk, and we are looking down from a ridge at a village in the middle of England. This, you will agree, is a place God meant to be admired, so completely do the hills surround it, not allowing us to concentrate on anything else. Our route has been worked out in considerable detail. 'First, at the ditch which Bishop Ælfic caused to be dug, then along the path to the wide track. Along the track to Helmstan's clearing . . .' Ah yes, I had forgotten to mention one thing. The walk we are taking is in the year 1021.

If you have a map, find Daventry, then the A45 to Northampton and the A361 to Banbury. Where these two roads form a right-angled triangle with the town, there, half-way along its hypotenuse and two miles from Daventry, you will find the village of Newnham. Just as for a moment in their lives a king of England, his queen, two archbishops, nine bishops, eight noblemen and seven abbots found Newnham.

The turnout implies a piece of PR, that day in 1021 when they all witnessed the charter by which Canute the conqueror, his wars behind him and anxious to get on the right side of the English Church, gave the village to the Prior of Evesham.

But it is not these grandees that concern us, it is the unknown men who had earlier walked the eight-mile boundaries of Newnham. A Saxon charter is not like the Domesday Book, which is a piece of accountancy; a Saxon charter is a historical record as it might have been kept by the Ramblers' Association of the Dark Ages.

The clouds roll back and you are on a walk in the open air. You are spotting landmarks. The deer's wallowing place. The spring among the willows, the deer leap. The dirty little stream. The brook. All these are mentioned in the Newnham Charter and some are there now, for the land does not change that much. The River Nene is small at Newnham (for the brook has acquired a name), flowing among willows along the southern boundary of the village. But forget the immaculate cottages and the burglar alarm, which on an evening in 1990 will sound for two hours.

You must imagine strips of land (for men have started clearing the undergrowth again) running to perhaps twenty huts of mud and straw, built here and there like things left behind after a flood. We are moving through them, west and then north, as the walkers did when they followed the sun, as was their custom.

We are taking their path up Newnham Hill, now a country lane, to Daventry. At the top is the cutting men still call the 'Deer's Leap', but no one has ever seen a deer leap it. Here we pause and climb a hill to the west to see whether there is anything left of what was mysterious to the walkers even then.

Ignore the sign 'Respect Trees' in front of a coppice, something which would have baffled them, for they would have been proud of their achievement in clearing this hill. It was here that they saw 'a heathen burial mound', a reminder of how old the land was in 1021. But there is no trace of this. To the north-east now, to Borough Hill, bristling with the transmission masts of the Overseas Service of the BBC. There was a Roman villa there but that had gone long before the walkers came. And we are beginning to move south, into fields and hedges, an agriculture that has erased their landmarks.

At this point a snigger reaches us across the centuries. The walkers came on two small rounded hillocks at this point with a trickle of water between them; these they called 'The Buttocks'. And, dutifully, the bishops and abbots recorded that the Buttocks were indeed one of the boundaries of Newnham.

No water now but, under the trees, the hills are small and rounded. So south again, past Leofsun's headland to the road they called Portstreet, and which the Department of Transport calls the A45. South, to the Nene and our beginning.

See them there for a minute: a king's officer, a monk puffing alone with a piece of parchment, someone carrying his ink, a gaggle of local worthies like Leofsun, who had assured them this was his headland, and Helmstan, who laid claim to a clearing 1000 years ago.

1990

Domesday Blisworth

A FEW MINUTES in a 30 mph speed limit, a blur of undistinguished houses, a pub, a church on a bluff, and then you are through and accelerating. No one in living memory has been seen to stop and talk in the middle of the High Street – people need the reflexes of a wild animal just to get across it. For the High Street is the A43 between Oxford and Northampton now, where once Gytha held these lands . . .

In 1086 an entire village of perhaps seventy people would have stood in the sunken track, drawn from their little huts and the immense open fields, when the news came of something amazing – strangers in Blisworth. They would have stood and watched the one man writing Blisworth's Domesday entry and the few bored soldiers. We do not know the names of anyone who was there that day (*it will not be until 1200 that we know the name of a Blisworth resident, its rector*). Nor should we be too surprised that the village survives (of 325 villages in modern Northamptonshire, only forty are not mentioned in Domesday; of those included, six have been deserted).

Before Domesday, its history is uncertain, but 900 years ago, on an unknown day, Blisworth was there, caught in the vast trawl of royal accountancy. It is known who Gytha was. She was the widow of the Earl of Hereford, one of the Saxon royal family and the one known athlete of the eleventh century. The Welsh had only to appear on his borders and there he was, moving east at great speed; he became known as Ralph the Timid.

In the great share-out in 1066 Blisworth was just one of thirty-eight manors in Northamptonshire which fell to William Peverel, one of the Conqueror's chief Norman followers. His castle was to the north, in Nottingham, and, his master intent on not allowing the formation of great regional power bases again, the villagers probably never set eyes on their lord. In the manor house in the High Street, long gone now, though the name survived until recently, in a 1930s brick house on the site, there would have been a tenant knight living like a huge weevil, between wars consuming the produce of the manor.

This, probably the area of the modern parish, was there to support the man in armour. The people brought corn to his mill; they owed him so many days' work; and they could not leave the manor without his permission. Nothing changed for them. They were in Blisworth as their fathers had been and their children would be, because of the law and because there was a stream and the stream turned a mill. So they worked in the three bleak fields from dawn to dusk, each field the size of a modern farm; their wives wove and made cheese; their children scared the birds away. Theirs was an intensely communal little world, dominated by agriculture and religion, their work interrupted only by the many church festivals. But over that would have been the nervousness of a society based only on agriculture.

Let us for a moment open another window on Blisworth: the published memories of old inhabitants. Eight hundred years have passed and it is 1885. The men still go out to the fields, though these have been enclosed for seventy years; they start at four o'clock in the morning; their wives pick up stones and weed; the children gather acorns for the pigs. Meat is rarely eaten more than once a week, meals consisting of bread and potatoes, suet pudding and skimmed milk. The man who made notes in 1085 would not have found much to surprise him.

There would, of course, have been a new landlord, but then landlords always came and went, as the gentry played out murderous musical chairs. Two generations after Domesday, the Peverels had gone, having chosen the wrong side in civil wars. It was an occupational hazard for the Norman fighting man, that and indigestion (the rich, as Aldous Huxley wrote, were prone to visions because of their high meat diet).

In 1485 another lord clanked out of Blisworth to another lost cause: Roger Wake fought for Richard III at Bosworth and duly had his manor taken away. But he bounced back, regained possession and now lies in state in the parish church. It was his son who sold out, breaking a line which had lasted for two and a half centuries, and at this point you might expect the first casualty, the last knight riding into the sunset. But descendants of the last knight rode back.

'We Wakes are a tough lot,' reflected Sir Hereward Wake, 14th baronet, in his estate office at Courteenhall, just a mile away. 'This time we came back 313 years ago.' The family had maintained its weakness for wars and losers, ruining itself in the Civil Wars until one married the daughter of a London merchant who had bought Courteenhall. 'We went in for every war that was going,' Sir Hereward brooded. 'None of us ever went in for trade or commerce. We always had acres and we never had money, though we did make the odd good marriage.' Heiresses came tripping over the parkland, and, in lace and silk, the old Norman fighting men survived. They have run out of space for plaques on the walls of their church, and a recently discovered fourteenth-century inscription now hangs in the belfry, the family tree in a bathroom.

Yet at sixty-nine Sir Hereward is aware that he has lived through more change than all the admirals and the generals on the church wall. 'I remember my father in an open car continually taking off his cap because people touched theirs off to him. They respected him for what he was, but not many call me "Sir" now. The war changed everything. I used to go to Blisworth in a pony and trap with my nanny. It was dusty and I can remember the pigs lying in the road and the horses shying from them.'

His father was a General, he himself started life as a professional soldier, but he describes himself now as a professional land agent and farmer, activities in which his son is now succeeding him. In the family history this is the biggest change of all. Roger Wake would have been outraged to hear himself called a farmer; you have only to look at 'villein', a social category in Domesday, now a term of abuse.

The Wakes were the last resident lords of the manor; after them lordship became grand and distant again. Blisworth was sold to the Crown and when Charles II assembled an estate for one of his bastards it became part of the Duchy of Grafton. With that all lordships ended, for in 1919 the Duke sold up. George Freeston, who has lived in Blisworth all his life, remembers the Great Sale, when the farms and cottages were bought, for the most part, by their tenants. The sexton bought his cottage for £50 and paid it off at a shilling a week; it took him all his life and is an example of the poverty which persisted in the villages of England.

But it was the Duke who presided over the first great agricultural change, when in 1812 Blisworth land was enclosed. It was an end to the old privileges of grazing cattle on common land: today no common land survives, and the farmers, who until the early nineteenth century had still lived in the village, bringing their cattle down at night in the old way, moved out and on to their land in the great farmhouses built by the Duke. Today there are five farms around Blisworth; out of a population of 2000 perhaps twenty now work on the land. This change would seem quite overwhelming to any of the ragged men and women who gathered around the Domesday commissioner. The former village farmhouses, mostly seventeenth-century and built in the old way, gable end to the road, survive; the prices they now fetch are the despair of the old people, pure joy to the young estate agents in the towns.

But another figure is still there, casting a long shadow back across the centuries. Harry Bunker is the 56th known Rector of Blisworth ('What brings it home to me is the way the steps in the church have been worn away'), but he is also the last resident incumbent in a line which stretches back 800 years. The next rector will be shared with other villages, as has happened all round Blisworth.

Domesday mentions no church or priest there. The church came later, its oldest part dating from the thirteenth century, its North door, as was customary, fronting the Manor. Medieval man would not find the church unfamiliar; he would recognise the clutter in the aisles, for children now get taught there, and there are blackboards and teacups and stacked chairs, the church in the late twentieth century returning to the old community church of long ago. What would bewilder him is that Mr Bunker preaches and conducts services from the nave; the mystery of God's vicar in the chancel, with the rood screen closed, is over.

One by one the old village tradesmen left: the smith, the wheelwright, the baker. When in 1918 the old bakehouse was closed, it was an end to a tradition which existed at the time of Domesday: the communal bakehouse around which village life turned. The mill survived into living memory, though the last water mill closed at the end of the eighteenth century. A windmill and then a steam mill survived until 1921 (medieval man would have been dumbfounded at that bit of news: the one reason for the village being there had gone).

But by then a lot had happened. The Grand Junction canal had come, and the Blisworth Tunnel, opened in 1805, was probably the most important single piece of civil engineering in British history: it linked the canal system of the North with that of the South, so that the Industrial Revolution floated through Blisworth. In 1838 the railway came, and Blisworth junction was the crossroads of England, Stephenson reflecting that while he could get a train into Northampton, he could not guarantee getting it out again, so for years Northampton was on a branch line from Blisworth.

The fascinating thing about all this is that at this point Blisworth *should* have become an industrial town. Iron ore was found there in 1852, in the hitherto unknown mineral-bearing county of Northants. It was the busiest canal port in the Midlands. There was the railway. And then, mysteriously, the moment passed. George Freeston accounts for it in this way: 'It was the dukes. They owned everything and they loved the land and they loved foxhunting. They wanted nothing to change.'

Blisworth is two villages today. There is the old village built along the roads; and there is the huge carbuncle of modern housing that came in three stages, in the 1930s, 50s and 60s, making an estate which now dwarfs everything else. More than a thousand people live there, most of whom work out of Blisworth. There is now just one big employer in the village, an abattoir with a staff of 200. It has become a dormitory village.

'I think it'll survive,' said George Freeston. 'The old people, they would never have complained about anything the Duke did. But these people, they organise petitions. I think that's one of the biggest changes I've seen. The man who moved in yesterday, he'll see to it that Blisworth survives.'

Much remains. A Miss Plowman still lives in the village where three centuries ago her ancestors carved their names on the largest house.

Candle Cottage on the canal was where canalmen bought their candles before going through the Tunnel. The Glebe Farm was the parson's private holding. Just names now, which once no one in Blisworth would have needed to have explained to them. Gytha held these lands . . .

1985

The House

I

THIS IS THAT longed-for day, once so far into the future it was not even a pinprick of light. It has been twenty years, longer than most life sentences for murder, and at the start we all speculate as to the form this day will take, for there were so many people there at the beginning. But at the end there is just you when you pay off your mortgage.

I thought there might have been some kind of ceremony when, like a colonial power, the building society went out of my life, perhaps not a slow furling of flags or bugles at midnight, but there might have been a chap in a suit buying me a coffee. Whereas there was only a letter and a signature I could not decipher, informing me it was all over between us. When the Roman army pulled out of Britain, at least the Emperor Honorius wrote instructing the inhabitants to look after their own affairs. When the Halifax wrote, it was just to instruct me to cancel my standing order. Then something odd happened.

If you want to know what it is like to pay off a mortgage, it is this: one morning your house fills up with ghosts. Until then it was easy to pretend to yourself that nobody lived here before you. You can't do this when the deeds come.

They came a fortnight later, and suddenly there they were, all the men who had owned this 'messuage or tenement', emerging from 200 years of documents like guerrillas come down from the hills. John Wooding, blacksmith. William Claydon, 'yeoman'. Good lord, I thought the yeomen of England had gone with Robin Hood. William Darby, builder. Charles Bartholomew, squire and harem proprietor. Frank Webb, his illegitimate son, a plumber. Reginald Chapman, postmaster. William Thompson-Coon, farmer. Parchment to paper, copperplate ('in the seventh year of the reign of our sovereign lord George IV') to typewritten page.

I call up John Wooding first. He bought and rebuilt the house in the boom time of the war against Napoleon, but in the slump which followed was forced to mortgage it. Eighteen years later, with not a penny paid off, his mortgagee, the yeoman Clayton, repossessed the house. Spare a thought for blacksmith Wooding who lived on here as a tenant, coming and going every day under the stone which bears his initials, those of his wife Mary and the date 1815.

It is 1909 and I call Charles Bartholomew, squire and sex maniac, who whenever he made one of the village women pregnant, installed her in a house. He bought many houses. 'I remember her well, the woman in your house,' said the oldest inhabitant. 'She was very ladylike and had a Pekinese. And every Sunday she had her dinner sent up from the hall. My God, I can smell that dinner now.'

Lastly, I call Frank Webb, the Squire's slip-up, plumber and much-loved village kleptomaniac. We have heard a lot about Frank and his little habit of taking away a souvenir from each job. Whenever my wife loses anything she blames him, though Frank has been dead thirty years. I always thought he had been given this house, but no, here are details of a sale in 1933, when Frank had to buy his father's house for £400. They tell you a lot about local history, these deeds; also about inflation, for in the 1820s the house had been valued at £200, dipping to £120 in the 1880s.

All these people crowding in, only one of whom I have met, Reginald Chapman, very old and stooped. 'Like Nebuchadnezzar I am coming down to the grass,' he told me. But Thompson-Coon, the man I bought the house from, I never met, though I once read an article about him in *Country Living*. I think he and his wife knitted sweaters or something.

II

T HE DATE-STONE first. Just under the eaves, this consists of the letter W, below which are two other letters, J and M, all three being above the figures 1815, the year of Waterloo. I had assumed the date-stone was an afterthought because the house had features which seemed to belong to an earlier time. For instance, there was the fireplace in the dining-room – a large inglenook with a chimney in which six men could have stood. No Regency structure that, so either country builders had gone on in the old way or the thing had stalked the fields like the Undead to leap onto any new house it found.

The first document explains this one, being a mortgage granted in 1826 by William Claydon to John Wooding, on the strength of the latter's house, referred to here as 'new erected'. So that accounts for the date: it was probably built in 1815, but there are references to it having been built on the site of a much older house. Now when this was done in the country, certain features were often retained if it was too much trouble to pull them down. This explains the chimney – they would have built the new house around it.

There is also an explanation for something else. When I bought the house there was a large stone building described as a garage in the garden. The only problem is that it has been impossible to get a car into this garage because of the apple trees planted in front of the door. Funny, I thought, and have thought since. But this, I learn, was a brew house – which goes somewhere to fulfilling my old dream of owning a brewery.

Wooding's mortgage was for £200 and the interest on it five per cent. But why should the blacksmith have found it necessary to take a mortgage out on a house he had built eleven years before? The infuriating legal gobbledegook gives nothing away, but what we are probably looking at is the victim of a recession that occurred long ago.

A blacksmith such as Wooding would have done well out of the agricultural boom of the war against Napoleon; with the exception of farm labourers, most people did do well in the country, which explains why yeoman Claydon had a few bob lying around, and why Wooding felt able to build a house this size. But Wooding would have been caught out in the post-war slump, when blacksmiths suffered the way garages are suffering now. We do not bother to have our cars serviced; our ancestors let the horse-shoes wear down.

And theirs was an even more implacable recession. A second deed, dated 1840, is a conveyance of this house, ironically still referred to as 'new erected', from Wooding to Claydon. After fourteen years, even though he was up to date with the interest, the poor old blacksmith had been unable to pay off a single pound of the £200 owing. Subsequent documents explain the letters on the date-stone, for they refer for the first time to Mary, Wooding's wife. When they were perhaps newly married in their first house, and the future seemed so assured they had their initials cut in stone. W, J, M. 1815. Poor things. John's signature, light and precise on the 1826 document, has become a tired scrawl by 1840. The cross that Mary set against her name is wobbly and uncertain, the mark of someone who not only could not write, but actually had difficulty holding something as foreign as a pen.

Still they survived. In a gazetteer of 1849 I find John still in business as a blacksmith. What happened to him I don't know, for in the last document he was not mentioned, as the house went for auction in 1884 at the village pub. This will make gloomy reading for those who still believe in property as an investment; the house fetched only £120.

But enough of gloom; we are almost into living memory and a very curious couple are awaiting their entrances: a squire with a toy railway and a real life harem, and his son. Francis Webb, plumber of this parish: 'He could fix any machine that went wrong. He made a little model tank once, out of brass, and the turret turned. Of course, it wouldn't have done to ask where the brass came from. When Frank moved into your house it took him a day – and a week by night, on account of his souvenirs. You know that garage of yours that you will never get a car into because of the trees Frank planted in front of the door? I saw inside it once and it was like Woolworths – racks of hammers and screwdrivers and taps. It was as though he needed something to remind him of every job he had ever done.'

I have one photograph of him. It is of a village outing, and among the schoolboys and the mothers there is one man who stands apart, a heavily moustached man with large, mild, puzzled eyes. The first time I saw that face I had the feeling I had seen it before.

'Of course you had,' said Doug Brown, the village grocer. 'Those eyes and that moustache were his father to a T.' Frank Webb, illegitimate son of the last squire. 'Old squire called on Miss Webb, his mother, every Wednesday afternoon for coffee. Got through a fair amount of coffee in his time, he did.'

Albert, now dead, told me about this first. 'Called on Frank one day and he was sitting with his back to the winder. "You ever seen this face before?" he said. "Well, I seen it on you," I said. "No, on anyone else?" he said. Course, then it come to me. "You're not one of his are yer?" And Frank nodded.'

Everyone liked Frank, in spite of his little weakness, but then he practised this weakness on such a scale as to pass beyond nuisance into farce. 'You couldn't even put mole traps down in the allotments if he was about. Come night, Frank would have them traps.' Like Ozymandias, King of Kings, Frank not only needed to reassure himself that he had passed this way, he needed others to know it too. He chiselled his initials into walls, and when Parish Clerk Weekley pulled his lavatory cistern away from the wall, there was the wild signature among the cobwebs on the plaster, F. Webb.

There was an enormous innocence to the man. 'Went past your house one evening and there was Frank up a tree, smoking his pipe. "What you doing up there?" I said. "Hard to believe," he said, "but you know that new bungalow? You can see right into their bathroom from here. She's having a bath at the moment." "Come down," I said. "They'll have the law on you." But Frank couldn't see how.'

John Butler once came upon him 30 feet underground. 'It was up in the fields and he was supposed to be cleaning out this well, only there was no sound of work being done, just pipe smoke drifting up out of the hole. "Hello," I shouted down. "Hard to believe," said a voice, "but from here a man can see the stars in daylight . . ."'

He loved trees and planted them all over the garden, so that no grass grows, just hazel, ash, elder, and so many varieties of plum and apple that we grow frantic in the autumn over what to do with them. We also wonder what became of the emporium of souvenirs, and think it has to be hidden somewhere, like Dark Age treasure.

Not long after we moved into the house, four elderly people called one summer afternoon and sheepishly asked whether they might be shown over the house. They quite understood if this would be inconvenient but it would mean a lot . . . It was Frank's nephew and he wanted to see for one last time the house where he had come as a boy and been happy.

During Frank's last illness, John Butler offered to look after his greenhouse for him. 'And that was a shock and all. The things I found. I came on my father's Bible with his name written in it. Oh, he was a one-off, was Frank.'

He never came back from the old folk's home, and was, I think, the first in the history of this house to die among strangers.

1995

PART TWO

A Field Full of
Folk: Absences

The Last Squire

I

H E WAS BURIED sixty years ago in the churchyard, under the cryptic epitaph, 'Peace, perfect peace.' It was only much later I came to appreciate that this could as easily have applied to the women of the village. But his photograph still hangs in the pub and they have not stopped talking about their last squire. The village historian wrote only the good things in his book, the water he brought to the village, the school he extended, the church he had restored in hard Victorian Gothic. You have to wear down his resistance before you hear the rest. The village historian is old enough to have remembered the squire.

'He used to have these open days down at the Hall, lots of drink and a marquee. They always ended the same way. He'd bang a drum and then he'd make a speech, always the same speech. "Trust in the Lord," he'd say at the end. "God save the King." Then he'd look round him and shout, "And keep your bowels open."'

But the historian is not keen to enlarge on the squire's other weakness. Albert is. Standing like a guardsman beside the bar, Albert remembered an early bewilderment in his long life. 'I never could understand why the village had no cricket team. Not enough players. Never come back from the war, I thought. But it weren't that. It was Squire.'

In the photograph the Squire's eyes above the Crippen moustache are troubled. He was old when it was taken but he still had the look of a man who had spent a lot of time trying to work something out and never had. 'Six maids he had down at the Hall,' said Albert, 'and not one was safe from him. His missus, she coulden take it in the end. Went off, car 'n' all, and nobody saw her again. Tall woman. Squire lived with his housekeeper after that. Called herself missus but he never married her. Mind you, he was good to the girls. When the children as shoulden have been come along, he'd set them up in a house. 'Course, he owned the whole village, barring about two houses. I remember those children, the others used to make fun of them. When they were old enough they went away and they never come back.'

The village historian, after much prompting, counted on his fingers. Yes, there had been so-and-so, and old Miss What's Her Name, and the farmer's daughter. He was well into double figures and could have gone on when he stopped. There were a lot of children, he said.

The Squire's other passion was railways. He had a miniature track laid from the village station to the Hall, with trains big enough to carry people. Once or twice a year he gave the village free rides on it, and in the pub photographs you can see the small hands waving flags in the open carriages. The railway is long gone, though you can still see the remains of the platform; in centuries to come they could baffle archaeologists.

I have this vision of the Squire, an old man in moonlight, sitting astride his engine, whooping softly as it goes in and out between the trees, his face as puzzled as ever.

He was not a local man. The money was made by his father up North in coal mines; having made it, he must have thought of seeing his son inch up the social ladder, so he bought him an estate in the South. The Squire never worked, probably never had the time, but he was good to the village. There was the water and the church and the school. There was also a fit of whimsy during which he castellated the ruined windmill. Apart from Albert, the villagers do not mention his weakness at all, and when they talk about him, it is as though he is not dead at all, but, like King Arthur, gone into a long exile.

The Hall was pulled down after the last war and the stone sold to builders. Only the stables remain and an avenue of trees leading from the two gatehouses; the drive has gone and a local farmer has turned the park into grazing land. But a few features remain. Among the rocks above a dried stream is a stone seat the Squire had built, an immense classical thing, the sort the gods sit on in illustrations to fairy tales. Here he must have sat, trying to work things out.

He attempted a pleasure garden here, building steps up from the bed of the stream, and concealing a stone crocodile in its depths. That might have been there to frighten some little creature and allow him to comfort her. Dried leaves and mud conceal the crocodile now. But there is something else, something very odd indeed. Two great urns are still there, each the height of a man. Carved out of a single block of red alabaster, each is of an ovoid shape.

'Here,' said Albert, a rare grin on his face. 'You ever thought what they look like?'

II

CHARLES BARTHOLOMEW (1851–1919) was an extraordinary, even tragic, figure. His father, a Victorian industrialist and friend of George Stephenson, bought the village for him in 1876. Just think of that for a moment. He bought all the houses – now lived in by admirals, accountants and company directors, and drooled over by estate agents. He bought the lot, with pubs and shops, as though all these were just Lego models for a playroom. This was, of course, the classic English paradigm of social advancement: far from the coal dust and the factories, his heir entered into his inheritance as a landed gentlemen. Charles was twenty-five.

And he had been given a complete little world, for the village then had butchers, coopers, wheelwrights, bakers, shoemakers, and was off all the main roads. But a hint of quiet poverty is given in one of the few old photographs, of twenty-six people, expressionless in bonnets and shawls, sitting outside a hall where they have just been given their daily free milk. That is what the old remember when they talk about Charles. He operated a sort of tiny welfare state and picked up the tab for everything. When times were bad, he had men knock down a wall or two, then had them build them up again. The village had never known anything like it. In the long line dating back to the Knights of the Hospital, the squires (John Dryden among them) had come and gone, and were forgotten. But nobody could forget a man who had given the cricket team its pitch and pavilion, the silver band its uniforms and instruments, and whose church clock is still to be heard chiming the hours all night long.

Still, largesse on this scale, even with the revenues of Wombwell colliery to underwrite it, is mysterious. Why should Squire Bartholomew have opened his coffers to these villagers? The answer is simple. As far as I can make out, Mrs Bartholomew was everything the young Charles needed, being of that class to which he aspired. But Mrs Bartholomew, on account of his interest in things biological, did a runner, whereupon Charles set up house with a blacksmith's daughter. She had been his housekeeper, and a photograph survives of a small, birdlike woman with a broad forehead. Before she took on her new responsibilities, Charles, who never did anything by halves, sent her to a finishing school in Eastbourne. They never married, although he had two children by her and she was known as Mrs Bartholomew. But what this meant was that they were cut off from the life of the county: no visiting cards were left and she never did have the chance to exercise her new social skills. So the village, apart from the odd trip to reassure himself that there was still coal in Yorkshire, also became Charles's whole world.

Everything had been made ready for guests, the Hall extended with a museum, which contained the legs of a bed in which Queen Elizabeth once slept, and the model railway had been laid through the park. Only the guests never came and the years passed. Charles played with his railway (for he was a qualified engineer, another odd detail) and with his cars (a founder member of the RAC, he was probably hurt more by the loss of his car than by that of the original Mrs B). He also showed a lifelong interest in one-parent families, of which there were suddenly many in the village. And then it was all over.

After his death there was a cricket match at which Bartholomew's son told the village grocer that he and the family were leaving and would never return. 'I don't need to tell you the reason,' he said. There was an eight-day sale and the Hall was demolished. Squire Bartholomew was the only one of his family buried here.

1985, 1993

Lord, Why Hast Thou Forsaken Us?

'LOST, MISSING or strayed, the Lord of the Manor of Blakesley in Northamptonshire. Anyone knowing his whereabouts, or even who he is, please contact Parish Clerk Weekly, The Great Lodge, Roaring River, Jamaica.' For ten years a village in the middle of England has been desperately seeking its lost lord. In the Saxon poem *The Wanderer* a lordless man laments his destiny: 'Where has the hero gone, the bounteous lord, the benches for feasting in hall?' But it was not destiny, it was the Charity Commissioners who forced Blakesley's quest upon its inhabitants.

Since 1913 the village hall had been run by trustees, whose election required all male villagers to vote, but for reasons of political correctness, it was decided to change this to allow a straightforward committee of management to run things; the Charity Commissioners were informed out of courtesy. A letter came by return. There could be no such change, it was pointed out, without the permission of one ex-officio trustee, the lord of the manor. *Who?* It was known there was a squire once, but he had been in the churchyard these eighty years. There followed a decade of appeals to Somerset House, interrogation of the old, and many frantic letters, and what made it even worse was that, after a recent auction, every hamlet in the neighbourhood had its own brand new leaping lord.

A lord of the manor writes: 'Once again I send you greetings, although I will not be able to be with you, due to a previous commitment in Arizona . . .' The letter appeared in this year's village fête programme at Maidford, two miles up the road. It had been sent by fax. Two years ago Steven Moore, an American pharmacist (with a mortar and pestle in his coat of arms), bought the title. Since then he has taken his duties seriously, contributing to church funds and appointing startled bailiffs, reeves and pinders. His seal hangs in many a tiled bathroom. 'And yet another spring arrives, with the promise that once again the earth will provide its ample harvest and residents continue in their daily routines . . .' See them pass singing to the fields, the accountants, bankers and estate agents of Maidford, scampering out of their hovels, 'when softe bene the wetres'. And suddenly nobody knows who is fooling whom.

The German Lord of Brackley, a doctor, this year gave £4,000 to the town's schools, and the Texan Lord of Coventry breezed into an inner-city pub to inform some out-of-town Jamaicans that he was their new Liege Lord. Not all are absentees. Ian Fisher, who runs the local taxi firm, bought the lordship of Moreton Pinkney, three miles from Maidford, for £11,000 just to keep it in the village, and at the auction met an ex-prostitute who was buying her title so she could open a hostel on the village green for her old colleagues.

But what amazes me is that so far politicians have shown no interest at all. The origins of the manorial system are in the crumbling Roman Empire, when the central power, hitherto absolute, had to rely on private military force. Thus great landowners were allowed to tax and police their tenants, even to conscript them for military service, and it was only the commercial union – which the Empire protected – that prevented the further development of the system. That had to wait until the Middle Ages.

Are you with me? The manorial system represents the last privatisation of all, that of the state. It was the earliest European Union that threatened its beginnings; it was the revival of state power and a tax-raising bureaucracy that finally destroyed it. The manorial system is the terminus of all right-wing political thought. So come home, John Redwood. The little house exists, dusty but still fully furnished, which could accommodate all your dreams.

But it is not the possible arrival of Mr Redwood that now terrifies the lordless villagers of Blakesley. Last month a letter came out of the blue from the Charity Commissioners, saying there were no more objections to the proposed changes. It had been found that the Lord of the Manor died in 1974. The letter did not say where this took place, or even who the man was, and the villagers, by now terrified of the Commissioners, have not asked.

1996

The Captain's Unusual Trophy

IN THE HALL is a single grey ear of great size. His first elephant, says the Captain modestly, shot in the Malay Peninsula. After that, the foxes' heads begin, followed by those of deer, elk, all the way up to the skulls of the great carnivores. The Captain has clearly killed his way around the world and, in the process, across the entire animal kingdom. Only the Captain has not stopped there . . .

Some of you may have seen the cartoon of a man with the Captain's moustache showing a guest his trophy room. Here, the heads hang in rows, each with time and place recorded. But beyond them, one head hangs slightly apart from the others, a plump, puzzled head in a World War I German spiked helmet. 'Somme, 1916.'

I used to laugh over that once; not now. But then until last week I had no idea that within living memory there were men loose in the shires madder than any of the great Tom Sharpe's creations. I had not heard of the Captain.

His name was Captain Pennell Elmhirst, educated at Rugby and Sandhurst, who, besides writing for the *Daily Telegraph*, was 'Brooksby' of *The Field*, the magazine's hunting correspondent. He lived at Blisworth House, Blisworth, in Northamptonshire, where foxhunting squires always lived until the last of them, a Colonel Clinch, broke his neck in the 1920s.

And it is October 1911. The Captain is showing a reporter from the *Northampton Independent* round his home, the occasion being his retirement from *The Field*. When the article appears, a photograph of 'Brooksby' will accompany it, of a mild-looking man in a gleaming top hat astride an even more gleaming horse. The Captain looks as though no doubts ever penetrated that neat skull, but there is no photograph of the reporter, or even a name; he is merely 'a representative'. I imagine a plump man perspiring in bowler hat and three-piece suit, for, despite their shared trade, the Representative knows his place and is uneasy. In his first paragraph he will record: 'It was gratifying to obtain "Brooksby's" courteous permission for a personal interview . . .' The Representative is under the impression that he has been granted an audience by the Pope.

Not that he asks many questions. As he pads behind his host through the passageways, the Representative is clearly seeing things through the Captain's own bloodshot eyes as he describes 'the heads of grand old foxes, with plates attached bearing inscriptions recording their last gallant run'. It has not been an unpleasant afternoon, for the Captain, at sixty-six, has been everywhere. It is just that, as Horace Walpole said of Admiral Anson, he may have been round the world but never in it. All the Captain can remember are the things he shot and the foxes his hounds killed.

Thus he was in Japan in 1864 when an entire British regiment was required to protect the Embassy from the Japanese people, the country having been opened up to Western trade a few years earlier. But what the Captain remembers is that he had to import a pack of harriers to hunt anything from fox and deer to red herring ('to which last ignoble pursuit they betook themselves when the chase diminished'). A country was being dragged out of feudalism while the Captain arranged drag hunts in the moonlight. He was two years in China, too, in its long Imperial sunset, but he is a little vague on that, for it has been a crowded life and occasionally he has to peer at the little brass plaques under the heads to remind himself.

The Captain has many views on few things. Motorcars, he says, will not interfere with the sport. On the contrary, they will allow people who hunt to go longer distances and belong to several packs. So, through the long afternoon, the Representative padding behind, the Captain unrolls his mind. They come to the dining room, where the enormous head of an elk reminds the Captain that he was in Colorado in 1897. To show its size, he has placed the head of a roebuck, also killed personally, beside it. Near to these is the skull of a tiger 'met face to face in an Indian jungle'. And it is then that the Representative sees something which afterwards he can only describe as 'a souvenir of a wholly different character'.

On the wall is a long hank of platted human hair. His host looks at it as modestly as he has looked at all his other trophies. A Chinese pirate, he says, caught red-handed. The Captain has remembered what he got up to in his lost Chinese years.

1997

The Old Farmer

H E I S A Northamptonshire man, farming in the village of Grimscote
as his father did before him and his son does now. He can see beyond
the neat hedges of his bungalow his old farm, and a few years ago, after the
death of his wife, he began to write his autobiography in neat longhand.
The pages were photocopied and he had them bound in a loose-leaf folder.
One hundred and fifty copies were made and he sold these at £5 each.
Their existence is known only by word of mouth, yet to the bungalow
come airmail letters asking for copies.

He grew up in a world of horses, two nags to drive to market, five
workhorses, two stallions and a pony for him to ride every day to the
grammar school in Towcester. The horses, he said, did not work on
Sundays. Everyone in the village worked on the land, 'except for one or
two who walked across the fields every day to make shoes at Ascote',
where now, when they needed labour on the farm, it had to be brought in.
Strangers, he said.

He remembered the blacksmith leaving the village; he was a boy of fifteen then, but it was an event of such importance he remembered it. He
remembered the excitement when the first machine, a binder, came; he
was twelve. Two horses drew it and another walked in front to turn it.
There were steam engines on other farms, but they were so heavy and
made such a mess that his father never used them. He did not think there
would ever be a world without horses.

In 1940 the first tractor came. They were all very wary of it: 'We used
to let the blooming thing run all the lunch hour for fear we shouldn't get
it started again.' His son had four tractors now. 'Perhaps it's three. I know
he could manage with three.' He remembered the breeds changing. The
pigs of his boyhood were all black and white, Gloucester Old Spot. In
1912 the first Friesian cows came to his grandfather's farm from Holland.

Now, as he said, he could hardly keep track of the changes, which was why he had written the book. There had been more changes in farming in the last twenty years than in all history.

The only new buildings he put up were in 1939, and then only to comply with the terms of the TB test certificate on his milking herd. Now he looked across from his bungalow at what seemed to be a small town (a farmer does not need planning permission for any buildings under 5000 square feet). His son had three times more buildings than he had in his time.

In his day the farm was self-sufficient, but now his son had to buy eggs, bacon and butter. The pigs had gone and the chickens. On other farms they had been rounded up like dissidents, so in country lanes you come on something like a Nazi death-camp in miniature, the bungalow where the commandant tends his flowers and, beyond the huts and towers which house 20,000 chickens, three to a cage, their beaks cut off, the last job at night is to clear away those that have died during the day. *Arbeit macht frei*.

A third of the farm was now arable. 'It's these fertilisers,' he said with awe. 'We just had farm manure. That's the greatest change of all. The cereals go up and up, and they don't need milking.' An old farm worker's wife had written to him, 'It was so different on the farm in those days. No smelly silage or horrid sprays and weed-killers. We looked on it as our holiday to be able to work in the fields in summer where the air was fresh and good.'

The fields had changed. From his window he pointed to a 50-acre field; that had been three fields in his day. 'I don't like it, but he's got to do it. You get a combine in a small field and it's all out of scale. You'd never get anything done.' He looked wistfully out. 'They're rich men now.' On the farm the stables were now used to rear calves and only one horse remained, ambling unshod because there were no blacksmiths near. It roamed the farm like an old soldier who had run out of wars.

1988

A Mason Forgets

HE WAS REPAIRING the church tower and, working alone, had
built his scaffolding inside it. Up there he was among the bells in a
cramped, dangerous place. What little light came through the slats was
barred with shadow, and his eyes kept watering from the ammonia of pigeon
droppings. So it was some days before he saw what seemed to be a word
carved in the wood of the bell frame. He scraped with his trowel and there
were more words until, reading with difficulty, he could make out this:

> *Whosoever see-th this frame*
> *Knoweth Joseph Kelchur of Wood End maketh same.*

There was no date, and although there were Kelchurs living in the village,
none of them had heard of a Joseph. But whoever had cut that verse knew
only one of his own kind would ever read it, for the squire would not have
climbed up there, or the parson. It was a ghostly handshake in the dark as
one craftsman saluted his successor across the centuries. This is the
mason's story.

It is not generally known that craftsmen are a secret society. They
gloomily recognise their own and each other's work (my father was the last
in our town able to turn a stair, and grew old in a time when nobody
wanted their stairs turned), and they leave messages for each other. This
was found twenty years ago under the plaster of a house in Stroud and
dates from the 1830s, when, had it been found, it would have landed
someone in serious trouble: 'Down with Kings and Queens and the
Aristocrats and all Tyrants.'

Craftsmen carve a mouse, as Len Clatworthy, the sculptor and carpenter, did during the renovation of Tewkesbury Baptist Chapel, believed to
be the oldest in the country. But he carved it under the stairs when the

architect wasn't looking and where only one of his own kind would appreciate it. Small protests, all of these, against a world in which no one remembers their names.

'My first job was on the railway,' said the mason. 'We worked with the blue bricks repairing old arches, Stafford Blues, strongest bricks ever made, withstood any vibration, yet they never absorbed moisture. If it rained or there'd been a frost, you had to stop work: the bricks just slid about. It was all right before the last war, we worked at our own pace then, but after that these chaps came along who were going to show us how it was done. Only thing was, they'd only ever worked with the common reds and we forget to tell them about the blues. There were arches falling down all over the place.'

The mason forgot other things, too. 'You ever notice how the stones in the church wall are flaking? A stone is grained like wood: you lay it so the grain lies flat, otherwise it flakes. But the council laid that wall. Saw them doing it and I must have forgot to tell them.'

To remember only made trouble. 'They had to cut away part of the churchyard for the job and this chap in the village, he got the topsoil off 'em. I was passing his house one day when I heard his dogs going mad. They'd found a skull in the soil and it had a long ginger beard. I told the vicar and I thought he was going to have a baby. He stopped the work and held a burial service over the skull. The old foreman said if he ever heard who told, he'd take a shovel to him.

'Of course, you couldn't help but find such things. I was laying a drain in the churchyard, and some chaps who were with me, they found a skull. Found them playing football with it. Never told the vicar that time. Put a ton of hard-core over it.

'How did I get started? I was working on that farm beside the church, milking cows one Sunday night when the old farmer put his head round the door. "Hey," he said. He didn't like talking much. "You have to go," he said. "Why?" I asked, I couldn't think of anything else to say. "Can't afford you," he said. And that was that.

'My mother was a washerwoman, my father a ganger. He told me about this apprenticeship on the railway, repairing the arches, and he got

£5 from an old village charity for apprentices. That paid for my level, plumb line, trowel and hammer, and I was on the railway from April 1936 to April 1955.

'I renewed the village station platform completely but no passenger set foot on it after I was done. The week after I finished they closed the station; I reckon they must have forgotten to tell me. There is an awful lot of forgetting in this world, have you noticed that?'

1996

The Slave

To the right of the porch, top-billing in any graveyard, there is this inscription on a tombstone in Culworth Church, Northamptonshire. 'In Memory of Charles Bacchus (an African) Who died March 31, 1762. He was Beloved and Lamented by the Family he Serv'd, was GRATEFUL and Humane and gave hopes of Proving a faithful Servant and a Good Man. Aged 16.'

This is exactly as it is written, the 'grateful' alone in capitals, which perhaps indicates some guilt on the part of his owner, also in the churchyard. But the owner is under an urn and pedestal the height of a man, the ivy so thick around it no inscription, not even a square inch of stone, can be seen. It is the slave's tombstone that has been recut.

This was what confronted members of a Northamptonshire black history group. Set up to find what had become of all those decorative little black boys who peer out of the background of eighteenth-century portraits, they had come upon references to the tomb in a records office. But when they located it they found themselves peering at the only legible inscription in the churchyard. Who had had this done?

The matter of the lost black population of Britain is a great mystery. Plucked out of the holds of slave ships for their looks 200 years ago, these boys and girls became fashionable accessories, the turbaned toys of the rich. When they grew up, it is known some stayed in service (Dr Johnson had a black servant), but what became of the others? Did they marry? Do they have descendants living in this country?

If so, it is possible some people today might not even know they have a black ancestor. A West Indian girl at Oxford told me about one family in which after many generations a child was born so dark, its startled parents called him Midnight. But then a brother came along who was even darker; him they good-naturedly called Five Past. But what if such a family existed in England, the members of which had managed to trace their ancestry? Having died at sixteen, it is unlikely that Charles Bacchus had descendants, but it is not impossible.

I first met Neville Cornwall of the black history group some years ago at a local fair where he had a stand. We fell into conversation, and Mr Cornwall, a retired schoolmaster, began telling me about the group, some fifteen strong, and the discoveries it had made. The most productive field, it has found, was the eighteenth century, when parish clerks robustly entered 'African' in their registers, thereby simplifying research. But there were also some strange, much earlier, instances.

Of the 298 skeletons unearthed in a dig of a third-century Roman site at Stanwick, three are thought to be of black people, one, from the artefacts found with him, of high rank. And then the parish registers came. Blatherwycke, 1773. 'William Scipio, Mrs O'Brien's Black . . . aged seven, baptised.' Guilsborough, 1683. 'A Negro youth, known here by the name of Titus, baptised.' Middleton Cheney, 1780. 'Mark Anthony, a black servant, baptised.' Note the classical names these exotic pets were given (the Spencers had a page called Caesar). There were even moments when they slipped out from behind their names, as at the grave in Blatherwycke of a black servant said to have drowned saving his master's life in 1836. 'Here a poor wanderer hath found a grave / Whom death embraced when struggling with the wave.' James Chapple, a slave who belonged to the Hattons of Kirby, also saved his master's life, and survived, being given a local pub as his reward.

And then there was Bacchus of Culworth. The mystery of the recut gravestone was solved when it was found that an American lady had paid for it. A Mrs Day was a descendant of the Lindsey family, once of the village, and research had already turned up the fact that a Sir John Lindsey had actually had a daughter by an African slave around 1763. But this turned out to be a red herring. The breakthrough came with an entry in the Haslebeach church register: '1754, a baptism. Charles Bacchus, a Negro belonging to Richard Bond Esquire, aged eight years.' So now they knew the owner, and from a description of the pedestal managed to find his tomb, in spite of the ivy, it being the only thing of that height in the graveyard. But what was Bond's connection with slavery?

A history group member, Paul Bingham, found the answer in the Middlesex Record Office, for there was a dispute over a will, Bond's daughter having fallen out with her uncles. And there they were, these uncles, Richard Bond's brothers, described as plantation owners in Barbados.

And the tomb? Mrs Day, when they managed to trace her, said she had had it restored in memory of her mother, who had been very interested in local history. I found this the saddest touch of all. In death, as in life, Charles Bacchus was the object of the whims of others.

1993

Singular Sacheverell

T HE *WHO'S WHO* ENTRY begins conventionally enough. He was born on 15 November 1897 and is the sixth baronet, who in 1948 did what sixth baronets might be expected to do: he became High Sheriff of Northamptonshire. So far the pianos have been tinkling in the carpeted rooms behind the trees, but with the next line the fields and the wide skies fall away. In 1960 he was given the freedom of the city of Lima in Peru. And then you hear the rumbling as the books go by, from *Southern Baroque Art* in 1924 to *For Want of the Golden City* in 1973.

'Have you written books?' he inquired delicately, as though asking after a disease. 'I have written eighty of them. That is a terrifying thing, is it not? Do you not think so?'

The small perfect sentences formed and faded: there were no abbreviations in his talk and no slang. He had written so many books, he went on, that now, having run out of reading material, he had begun to read his own. It did not help him sleep. He alternated between pride and despair, he murmured, and in the end had to resort to a sleeping pill. What sort did he take?

'A yellow one,' said Sir Sacheverell Sitwell.

The house stands behind trees and walls in the village of Weston, near Banbury. Various owners have played with it, so that in one wing it is a cottage and in another a large nineteenth-century rectory. There are lawns and gravel and a small hump-backed bridge. The one man who did nothing at all to it was Sir George Sitwell, who could not keep his hands off any of his other properties. 'I don't intend to do much here,' he once said airily, 'just a sheet of water and a line of statues.' But nothing came of this. Instead, the house passed to his second son on his marriage, intended, wrote Anthony Powell, as Sacheverell's country living. He has now lived in it for over fifty years; his wife died here two years ago.

The house has been in the family for as long as anyone can remember. 'Old aunts, great-aunts, that sort of thing,' said Sir Sacheverell. His father, he remembered, had once told him that he heard his own great-grandfather, wounded in the Peninsular War, groaning in one of the rooms. The wild Regency face is on the wall, above the red coat and the epaulettes. 'Interesting face, do you not think?' inquired Sir Sacheverell.

He himself is a very tall, thin man. 'I was 6 foot 3,' he said wistfully. 'Now I doubt whether I am 5 foot 11.' He is also an extremely good-looking man, with one of those long, fine faces that writers of romantic fiction award their aristocratic heroes. He sat in an armchair, smoking, his legs tucked under him. He was polite but not particularly interested in answering questions. But then at eighty-five, who would be? So on occasions the perfect sentences disappeared into the thick carpet between us and the long face turned to the fire. But once or twice something caught his fancy.

In Isfahan he had seen the skeleton of a beggar 8 foot 6 inches long. Would not that be alarming to see, he ventured, a man of 8 foot 6 inches advancing to beg from one? And he had heard that in a town on the Somerset coast – Weston-super-Mare, that was it – there was the skeleton of a two-headed beggar, who had once met Charles II, he believed. That, said Sir Sacheverell, would be even more alarming. He had been twice to see the two-headed beggar but the place had been shut on both occasions. Yes, he agreed, he probably did have a taste for the bizarre.

Yet earlier he had reacted a little sharply to a suggestion that he was fascinated by torture and public executions. What executions? he said. Well, in *For Want of the Golden City* there were the accounts of men hung in cages, and the man broken on the wheel, with the old crone handing her executioner son his hammers, and the sounds. 'Terrible, terrible,' said Sir Sacheverell. He has written so much that he needs to be reminded of his own books. *For Want of the Golden City* is one of the loveliest, a guided tour through a man's mind, his memories, the places he has visited and the books he has read.

'I never had to earn my living, you see,' said Sir Sacheverell. 'I had a private income which was never large enough, but it did mean that I was able to indulge myself in writing about what I wanted to write about.'

The image you retain from *For Want of the Golden City* is of a man sitting in a library with the heavy curtains drawn. He writes about Angkor Wat and the temples of Mexico, but not about the village outside his window, which leaves you with the suspicion that Sir Sacheverell knows more about Angkor Wat than he does about Weston. 'I think things have changed here,' he said. 'One is aware of people having wirelesses. I think probably they stay in more.'

Was I aware, he said suddenly, that there were 1000 million Chinese people in the world? Was that not appalling? And he had once met a man in a lift who had told him that there were now 10 million people living in Mexico City. Had I known that?

There was not, someone once wrote, a remarkable landscape or a work of art or a building that Sir Sacheverell had not seen. He travelled twice a year with his wife, once in the spring and once in the autumn. 'I'd just decide where I wanted to go, and then get there,' he said. In the summer there was London, and then, when the days were drawing in, there was Weston again. It was here that the books were written; he wrote every morning, walked every afternoon, and then wrote again for two hours every evening. His housekeeper, Mrs Stephenson, and her husband, who acts as his chauffeur, have been with him for 104 years between them, he calculated. They moved with him from Derbyshire.

'I spent my childhood at Scarborough. Do you know Scarborough? And Whitby? Did you know that Dracula landed at Whitby? Why he should have chosen that, I don't know. Do you?'

He talked of his family. He had, he thought, a calmer temperament than either his brother or sister; he had not been involved in their rows. 'I did feel part of a trio. I think I first felt that when I was eighteen and at Eton. I suddenly felt close to them. Did you go to Eton?'

In his brother Osbert's autobiography their father, Sir George, emerges as one of the most hilarious eccentrics of the century (in his *Who's Who* entry he solemnly recorded his greatest achievement: 'Captured a spirit at the headquarters of the Spiritualists, London, 1880'). Osbert, said Sir

Sacheverell, had not been altogether fair on Papa; he had made him into a guy. Had he ever talked to him about this? Oh, yes, said Sir Sacheverell, he had remonstrated to some mild extent.

He was employed on just one occasion, when in the early 1950s he wrote the Atticus column for the *Sunday Times*. The pieces have been published ('and very amusing they are, though I say it myself'). No, he had not interviewed anyone during that time. He had just sent the articles off by post once a week ('anything I could think of that was interesting'). One day his editor took him to lunch and told him how much he enjoyed his writing; the next day he sacked him.

He was very interested in food, and in drink. He hoped I was too. No, he had never cooked; he had not even boiled an egg. Was that not strange? Well, there it was, he said sharply. But Mrs Stephenson was a frightfully good cook.

Now there was music (he had a great many records), and there was television. He had enjoyed *Fawlty Towers* and something with the very intriguing title of *It Ain't Half Hot Mum*. In *Who's Who* he had given his one recreation as 'Westerns', though that was a joke. But he did love Westerns: the ruffians and the heroes and the horses. And there was this frightfully good actor, Wayne, was that his name?

There were walks around the garden, and once a week there was shopping in Banbury. No, he had never set foot in the local pub in fifty years. But he felt that he was just existing now, especially after the death of his wife. 'You try being eighty-five, you will not like it very much. I never thought I would live this old. You don't. I think I feel about sixty, and I'm determined not to give in to it. I fear loss of memory.'

Then he brightened. His godmother had died aged 107. In her youth she had been sculpted by Rodin and in extreme old age *The Times* had written about her, giving her age as 179; that made her very cross and she died soon after. He loved misprints. There was one, he recalled, about the Salvation Army: 'Long after the audience dispersed a huge crow remained on the platform singing "Abide with me".'

Then it was time for drinks. Was it too early? Would whisky and soda do? From their frames the ancestors stared out. No, that was not a judge;

it was a Chancellor of the Exchequer. He was so relieved it was not a judge; judges had to sentence women who smothered their children.

Bernard came to draw the heavy curtains, and the fire flared in the open grate. Where did the wood come from? Oh, locally. But where?

Sir Sacheverell looked curiously at his guest. 'From trees, you know.'

1982

PART THREE

A Field Full of Folk: Presences

The Gentry Open Their Homes

A HOUSE SO VAST and old, it contains every building style from the Middle Ages on, so the baroque here is a mere incident as the decorators came and went. Another house where the portraits hang frame to frame, but each is of a horse, and man appears by accident. Houses never let, never sold, houses to which the general public has never before been admitted . . .

With summer just off stage, the Squire was honing up the commentary he would deliver when strangers trooped through his door. Francis Sitwell of Weston Hall in Northamptonshire, so rubicund and with eyebrows so dramatically upswept he could appear without make-up as the demon king in any panto, was up and running in front of a Press party. Within minutes he had informed them that his aunt Edith had died a virgin, waved his hand vaguely at a Jacobean sideboard, a masterpiece of the cabinetmaker's art ('the usual oak furniture'), pointed to his title deeds hanging on the wall, and held out the delights of the village pub to which, he said wistfully, they might all soon repair. There are guides voluble, guides respectful, guides stunned by the sheer weight of other men's possessions, but never a guide like this. 'It is an excellent pub,' pleaded Sitwell. It is also one that in the seventy years he lived at the hall, his father, Sir Sacheverell, never entered.

But the world beyond the park gates has changed. 'Through a Stately Key Hole,' an initiative by the Northamptonshire Chamber of Commerce, is offering: 'A unique opportunity to enter apartments, rooms, galleries and other areas . . . within historic family residences not normally open to the public.' Last year the owners of twenty-eight houses were approached, of whom fifteen nervously held back for reasons of security, which is another way of asking the question, what would be left in the other thirteen at the end of the season? But this summer six more of them have decided to sign up.

Some have known parties before, but these were fine art societies or learned groups, precise people capable of correcting a chap about his porcelain. It is the general public they all fear. 'People about whom we know nothing, or even why they're coming,' said Alastair Macdonald-Buchanan, of Cottesbrooke Hall, Cottesbrooke. 'You hear terrible stories about these chaps scuttling down your drive with vast bronzes under their raincoats.'

All visits are by prior booking, and then only with a letter of confirmation from the Chamber itself. This, in its way, is almost a return to the old Victorian tradition whereby anyone who applied to see a stately home, and looked like a gentleman, was allowed in. But now, unlike then, the family is often in residence. It can be poignant if you live locally, for these are houses you have only glimpsed from afar, or from footpaths in the case of the largest house of all, which does not even want to be named.

Walls behind walls, and towers behind them: the sheer weight of stone in The Big House With No Name is extraordinary, and what is more extraordinary is that it is not framed off by the landscape. You walk down a footpath and there is this mass of masonry that has been added to, and added to, down the centuries, starting with the medieval undercroft. This survives, if overlain, a barrel ceiling and panelling being added at the end of the seventeenth century, and this panelling painted to look like marble in the 1840s. The house has been owned by the same family for something like 1000 years, give or take the odd cousin, and everything that was fashionable at the time got added. It is a complete anthology of building and of interior decoration. Having been never rented or sold, or been the recipient of any public grant, here social change is something its owners may have glimpsed beyond the gates. That something like this can still exist, on its own terms in our time, will be a shock to many. It is now someone's second home.

Back at Weston Hall, meanwhile, a journalist admiring a bowl of dried flowers breathed to Mrs Sitwell, 'You've actually *grown* these?'

'Yes.'

'Have you really?'

Her wonder could not have been greater had Mrs Sitwell said she had knitted them. But then it affects people in different ways, this meeting the gentry. Some fall back on long-forgotten deference, others are off-hand to the point of rudeness, although none of it will have worried Francis Sitwell, energetically rubbishing his ancestors.

'*This was a very evil man.*' The calm face of an eighteenth-century politician stared down on the dining room. 'You must admit, he looks very unpleasant,' insisted Mr Sitwell before turning his attention to 'an awful-looking woman'. Then there was the Colonel, his own great-great-grandfather, who fought at Waterloo; but it was not this which interested Mr Sitwell. The Colonel, he said delicately, had had many romances, but he then began to reel off a catalogue of women, including the notorious Pauline Bonaparte, an essential pit-stop in the career of any self-respecting early nineteenth-century lecher. The longer the inventory of iniquity, the prouder Mr Sitwell seemed of his ancestors.

But he was startled last year when one of the visiting public announced that she was a Potocki and thus a descendant of one of the Colonel's lost loves, a Polish aristocrat. This lady in old age wanted to leave him her estate, but his wife would have none of it. 'Pity,' said Mr Sitwell. 'It wouldn't have been a matter of acres, but of square *miles* of Poland.' He looked around him. 'And if you can bear to stand here for a moment . . .' In Weston on a spring morning this proved difficult, as the cold indoors was that of a limestone cave, but Mr Sitwell did not notice. He showed us Edith's clothes laid out on a bed, including the gold brocade dress straight out of Aladdin, in which, he said glumly, she had turned up to take him as a boy to see *My Fair Lady*. It was a long time ago, but he had not forgotten the horror.

The house, he said, had been in the hands of the same family since 1714, and he showed us a line of bells that once summoned servants. Were there any servants now? None, he said, except for a cleaning woman and a part-time gardener. The past ten years, said Mr Sitwell, with feeling, had been a time of unremitting toil for his wife and him. Why, they did not even have a cook.

'Can we see the kitchen?' asked someone.

'No,' said Mr Sitwell.

And then it was all over and we were in sanctuary. 'Morning, Francis,' said the landlady of his local pub, who last year when such a party had assembled there before a visit had rung him in some alarm to say that one of them, a lady, appeared to have left all her underwear in the lavatory.

1997

Death at Christmas

THIS HAPPENED at Christmas. There was a dinner party in the course of which the host suddenly got to his feet and said, 'You must excuse me, I have a cow about to calve.' It is not an announcement you will hear over the gleaming Agas of Kensington and Chelsea.

The drama might have been undercut by his wife's sardonic enquiry as to whether he was still capable of distinguishing one end of a cow from another, but there was enough of it to send me stumbling after him into the night to witness the wonder of birth.

I have known the farm since I was a boy, and can remember when the family came, walking their cows along roads when it was still possible to do this. They did not have electricity here then, so you crossed the yard with a hurricane lamp, the night hissing and swaying around you, and there was a flare-path of cats' eyes, only these were real cats, one of them so wild it ran up the wallpaper when it ventured indoors. And there were whitewashed barns and byres in the corners of which, on heaps of straw, the family dachshund tried to assert her authority over sheepdog puppies already bigger than she was, scuttling off in a huff when this had no effect. The farm was a magical place to me.

But the barns and the byres are gone, pulled down to make room for two huge sheds, in one of which the farm machinery is kept, in the other the milking cows. 'You'll find the cowshed very different,' said my host. 'Remember how we used to keep the cows in their stalls from winter into spring? They're in a sort of dormitory now.'

Huge heads turned as the lights came on, at least a few did. Most did not bother and went on with the enormously serious business of eating or standing or lying down. Not one got out of our way.

You can tell what a farmer is like within minutes of seeing him among his animals, and it is sad to be in the company of someone at whose approach the heads jerk and there is blundering panic. Here we had to push our way through, and even then the cows moved slowly. He knew their names, for some were the children, some the grandchildren, of cows here in his father's time, and he was not unaware of the sadness of creatures stuck in perpetual cycles of pregnancy and lactation. 'All I can do is make their lives as comfortable as I can,' he said. 'Until they leave here, that is.'

It all starts here. We have all come from the land, yet it takes some vast disaster to remind us of this. In the late fourteenth century, following the Black Death, which had killed off between a third and a half of the population, there were suddenly poems in many languages about the fact that the whole edifice of life rested on the shoulders of the man in the field. *Pab nac ymerawdwr heb hwn,* wrote Iolo Goch, the Welsh poet: 'No pope or emperor without him'. In our time the land for most of us was virtually a foreign country from which occasionally we heard reports. We argued about its subsidies and its methods, but it was still remote. And then suddenly it wasn't. The land is a war-front now.

The farmer and I had pushed our way to the last pen of all, in which a cow was licking a small trembling thing that was trying to rise to its feet. 'You clever old girl,' said the farmer, going into the pen. She looked on as he examined her calf. 'Perfect,' he said at last. And it was, a perfect little creature, half-an-hour old. 'It's a bull calf,' he said to me. 'It has seven days to live.'

Because of the BSE scare, at the end of that time it will be taken away, shot with a humane killer, then incinerated, and the farmer will get an agreed compensation payment of £72. But that at least is something. For some reason there are no similar arrangements for those female calves not wanted for rearing, and two days later at the local mart, five were sold for 35p the lot.

'Do people know about this?' the farmer asked me. 'They see protests at ports, but that's all. This seems to be some huge secret we have to live with.'

We walked back to the house and did not speak again about the birth at Christmas.

1998

The Good Life

I

GEORGE, A MORTGAGE controller, and his wife live with their four little boys in the village, where they keep the post office. They also keep two goats, five sheep, 150 chickens, two pigs, eight rabbits, eighteen guinea-pigs, two gerbils, two budgerigars, four cats, two dogs and a gold-fish, with a donkey called Crystal about to join the Ark. They have one field, yet they produce and sell their own milk and free-range eggs. They rear their own pork and make their own cheese.

The mortgage controller is much in demand as a speaker at Women's Institute meetings; he addresses audiences of puzzled farmers' wives on 'The Good Life', and is a source of great diversion, especially when the family estate car, its back seat full of goats and pigs, passes to market. The one surviving link to the farming past, he is aware of the ironies. A new-born kid was called Lady Miras, as he had spent most of the year agonising over Mortgage Income Relief at Source. It has become his role to provide comic relief for country life.

'The goats came first. We bought them in Derbyshire after reading an advert in *Exchange and Mart*. Well where else do you buy goats? We told the woman we'd hire a trailer to collect them. Trailer? she said. They'd always gone in the back seat of the car. So we got them in the car, and they pid-dled all the way from Buxton to Blakesley.'

That was fifteen years ago. The pigs came next, for something had to be done with the surplus goat milk: the pigs drank it and grew. Then the hens came. He has become very fond of his hens, talking to them for hours about mortgages. The family keeps the sort of hours farmers once kept, getting up at 5.30 a.m., he to walk the dogs, feed the hens, pigs and sheep, his wife to milk the goats.

Some things they discovered the hard way, as when he turned his back on a donkey and was propelled headfirst into a basket of eggs. Then there were the dying pullets. He kept increasing their food and they kept dying. A clear case of starvation, said the vet, handling the tiny bodies. The pullets appeared to be eating them out of house and home when one morning, in the hard light of dawn, he saw a goat called Buttercup stealthily slide open a panel in the roost.

He takes goats' milk with him to the WIs ('Oh, Doreen, I couldn't.') The farmers' wives question and giggle and go red as he warms to his denouement, the Great Mating. 'We'd been told that goats did come into heat. They wagged their tails, we were told, made slight noises and were a bit restless. RESTLESS? The thing had smashed its way out of the shed and was bellowing like a rugby player kicked in the crutch. So we got it mated. And in a field I saw it, this thing the size of a Shetland pony with steam coming out of it, and we had this lovely thing like a gazelle. I covered her eyes.'

Children love their house. They learn startling facts, as that now under two per cent of all eggs produced in Britain are free-range. They see small things born. To the mortgage controller, coming home is like passing through a space-lock. The pinstripe is hung up and a pair of trousers that could stand unaided are put on. One hundred and fifty hens live in Blakesley and know as much about mortgage tax relief as any accountant. Local agricultural advisers shake their heads. Farmers grin. But they are all his customers.

II

THIS IS A report from a war front. It is dark and we are treading carefully; George has with him a torch, a pail and a dishcloth. As we near our objective, he places the torch and the cloth in the pail to move the plank aside with one hand, and we hear the first soft cluckings of alarm. George, with 100 free-range chickens, is preparing to hold the line against salmonella. He is a worried man.

From the Ministry of Agriculture the three leaflets have gone out, *Lay One*, *Lay Two* and *Lay Three*. The tone is peremptory, if panicky: '*The Poultry Laying Flocks Order 1989* replaces *The Testing of Poultry Flocks Order 1989* and *The Poultry Laying Flocks Order 1989*.' Only revolutionary governments have ever legislated at this speed.

The orders affect anyone who has a chicken and has sold a single egg, even to friends. From this year on, all will be required to take faecal samples or cloacal swabs from their hens. The battery death camps will have it easy, for a sliding scale applies with a cut-out at sixty hens per flock, so that if you have 10,000 hens you will still only need to test sixty, but if you have twenty you have to test the lot. Also, a farmer will only need to put his arm into the battery cage, test the hen and replace it. It is with the free-range flocks that a lunatic comedy intrudes.

George is writing a letter to the Ministry of Agriculture. He is pointing out that the only time he can catch his hens is at night when they come into roost, but if he then switches the lights on, they assume it is morning and run around. So it means he will have to steal in upon them, torch in one hand, pail in the other, swab in a third. He will also have to catch the hens. At the present stage of human evolution, George helpfully points out, a man only has two hands.

Again, he notes that when it comes to faeces, the Ministry stipulates that this has to be fresh. 'And how fresh is fresh?' George cries aloud like Wittgenstein in his despair. 'Is the morning after the night before sufficient, or do I have to spend my days loitering in the fields with intent?' And how does he send the samples? First- or second-class post? George's wife keeps the village post office and he has experience of Brie at dawn when the cheese has been held up in the post. Also kippers, says George. And in what sort of packet does he send it? The bureaucrats have specified that only a gram is needed, and with an airmail letter only 20 grams in weight, wild avenues of mischief are opening for George. For 37p he could send twenty individual samples of chicken shit to Mongolia.

A week later the Ministry replies. The letter is humorous but not practical. 'The sample should reach the laboratory for testing within two days, as we like to play around with the fresh sticky stuff rather than the dry crumbly stuff which falls through our fingers.'

So it is night. And two men, stealthy as paediatricians, are groping among the rafters of the chicken house. The next moment all hell is let loose in Middle England.

III

IT IS NOW five weeks later. Had he not used red Biro, the notice would have read like something hung on some palace railings after the royal gynaecologist had called. 'We are pleased to say that laboratory tests on our poultry, carried out under government legislation, have confirmed that they are free of salmonella.' George printed the word a second time, then underlined it.

The difficulty of collecting hen droppings led George to contact a friend who suggested an independent laboratory in Woking; they explained things better there, he said. So George rang up and heard a bright voice say that the first thing to do was to line his henhouse with white paper. George sat down at that point. The larger of his two hen-houses is 24 feet by 15 feet, and he was being told to turn it into a fashion photographer's studio. He heard himself ask, was there no alternative? There was.

You may find what follows indelicate, just as war is indelicate once the parades are over. Salmonella disappears from the news columns, but, in darkness all over this country, men are being abruptly introduced to the anatomy of chickens. George was advised to try cloacal swabs, was sent some and with them a line drawing which, as he said, could have been either a strange new shrub or Humpty-Dumpty looking extremely cross.

Armed with these, he tiptoed out to the henhouse and the sleeping hens a second time, and here he encountered a new problem. In real life a hen resembles neither a strange shrub nor Humpty-Dumpty. In real life there is a great deal of feathery fluff and cover. '*Whooooof*.' George blew desperately into the white swirling mass, which was beginning to struggle. The next moment the swabbed was squawking and the unswabbed, all by then awake, were running frantically for cover. 'And once they're on the floor, it's not a case of that's Gladys, and that's Gwen, and we've still got to do Amy,' he reflected, 'they all look alike.'

Somehow he did it. He swabbed thirty-five, sent the samples away, and then there was all the apprehension of awaiting an exam result. When that came, George had to stop himself going out to offer individual congratulations to each graduate under the trees. But at the same time he has had to recognise that nothing will be the same for him again. He had once thought of building up his flock, of even starting a hatchery; once he assumed his little egg business might be a lifeline to him in his old age. Not now.

It is Russian Roulette in Middle England now, and in three months George will have to spin the chambers again, this time to test the hens in his other shed. Yet these will have mingled with the others in his paddock during the day. His children, shooing them in at night, may have chased a few into the wrong shed, and some, giving way to whim, may have roosted with the goats or in the pigsty or among the logs.

Yet if one, just one, has a trace of salmonella, then the whole lot will have to be slaughtered. A million birds have already gone in this country. The procedure is open to abuse. George could keep a dozen apart like royalty, testing them over and over, for the Ministry does not visit.

And the regulations do not apply to imported eggs. If George went into the packing business, merely putting eggs from overseas into boxes according to their size, he would be spared the cycles of anxiety four times a year. Those boxes would not say that the eggs had been imported. What will come of it all? He asks the question and, like a jesting Pilate, does not answer it. For though salmonella will not be stamped out, it is quite possible that in our time men like George will. Yet on television, the politicians in the pinstriped suits who appear not to draw breath, talk on and on and have no doubts.

This began quite amusingly, did it not?

1988, 1994

Demolition

I DROVE PAST the other day and the bulldozers were in. The block containing the three garages had gone, and the wall round the house was 18 inches shorter. The appeal had gone to the Ministry, been dismissed, and the District Council was finally exercising its planning authority. Versailles is a little smaller now.

This is the story of a country lane, the smallest, narrowest lane you can imagine, barely a quarter mile of it running between fields, with cars hesitating at the sight of each other like strange dogs. Nothing else at all, except that two and a half years ago there was a cottage on the bend. An old lady lived there with fourteen cats which had killed everything except a solitary hen, and this, unhinged by its experiences, tottered from verge to verge. The cats, with nothing left to murder, lay at night in the hedges. They went first, carried off by flu, and suddenly the rabbits were back, bouncy and aimless, a revolutionary army spilling into the suburbs. Then the hen went, and finally the old lady, and the estate agents came, reaching deep into their word-hoards for a house which had no sewerage, no bath, no gas, no hot water. 'Totally rural,' they purred.

People came from miles around, for this was an opportunity to move back in time, into a world of mangles, bricked boilers and hydraulic hand pumps. Even so, the auction was a shock. There was some land with the house, two acres of brambles, and the agents priced it at around £60,000. It made £110,000, and after that I thought nothing would ever surprise me again about that place. But down the road *he* was coming. Sir John Vanbrugh, three centuries on and still dreaming of Brobdingnag, the Man Who Loved Big Houses. He came with planning permission to extend the cottage. He extended it all right: he built Versailles in the lane.

Behind him trundled the convoy bringing stone from the whole corner of the quarry he had bought. Now an average house requires between 70 and 100 tons; down the lane came 2000 tons of ironstone, and after this the computerised heating system, the insulation and the interlocking tiles that no winds would ever dislodge.

I knew nothing of this at the time. All I knew was that I passed one night and the cottage was gone; a month or two later it was up again, built of new stone, and a few months after that there were wings leading from it, and courtyards, and a balcony.

I became obsessed by the house. I would often stop to stare, wondering what would come next. What made it so extraordinary was that there were no drives leading to it, no park to frame it, just this vast bulk of stone crouched there in the moonlight.

And then one night the builder was there. I asked him why he was building this big old house; nobody wanted big old houses now. 'Aha,' he said, 'this is a big *new* house.' He was thirty-six years old, his beard was white, and since his twenties he had loved big houses. To him, he explained, a house was a sequence of doors, with a surprise behind each one. An indoor swimming pool under an arched chapel roof, a gymnasium lined with mirrors, an inglenook with a stone cut to resemble suede, a sauna bath. Surprises.

Ten years he had been building such houses, each one getting bigger and bigger, and this one in the lane was to be the biggest of all, with seven bedrooms and five bathrooms. 'My downfall is that if the site allows it, I just go ahead.' He saw himself as a man hung about with constraints, for the man who loved big houses was now up against something Sir John Vanbrugh never had to face with Blenheim. Yes, they said thoughtfully at the Planning Office, the cottage had been extended 'quite significantly'. And finally they had been obliged to act.

He had never thought it would come to this, said the builder. And the stones were such beautiful stones. The house still stands but now without garages, sauna or swimming pool – all the little surprises. As someone wrote after Vanbrugh had gone:

Lie heavy on him earth, for he
Laid such heavy weights on thee.

It had been a lesson to everyone, said the Planning Officer.

1990

The Day of the Rude Mechanical

I ASKED HIM ONCE where he bought his trousers. Florida, he said. It was a moment, which occurs perhaps once in a man's life, when he realises he is a witness to social history. He got all his work trousers there, he said.

Last week the Rural Development Commission published a report on life in the country. There has been a drizzle of such reports in the past few years. With shops closing, and 75 per cent of parishes without a bus service, life in the country, we are told, is a slow drawing-down of blinds. And then through the blinds he bursts, a man dressed in two sweaters, once the property of the German Army, and work trousers bought in America. 'Las Vegas I have never liked, but did you know that Chinese food in San Francisco is half the price it is in Towcester?' Country characters of the late twentieth century: the Village Mechanic.

Those of you who live in towns rarely meet a mechanic. They exist somewhere behind the potted plants and the smiling girls in black stockings who hand you a computerised bill, at which point you no longer notice the plants or the black stockings. But in the country, not only the school run and the social world, but all forms of employment revolve around one man. And in 1998 I am standing under a calendar on which it will be forever September 1993, the photograph for that month being that of a naked girl on a lawn among water-sprinklers. On other calendars, provided by motor-factors and tyre firms, time has similarly stopped on other months and other girls, all of whom I feel I know.

'You do realise you now have the perfect car,' says a man who has just eased a fifteen-year-old Sierra through the Stargate some call the MOT. 'Nobody's ever going to want to steal that.' The Mechanic can fix anything. Golf buggies, tractors, Reliant Robins, two-stroke and four-stroke, turbo and diesel, even Citroëns. Some of these, like the girls, lie around in various states of undress. If you turned up here with a Stealth Bomber, this man would not turn a hair.

'My favourite car? Haven't got one. A car's a car. They haven't changed much over fifty years, apart from the electrics.'

Somewhere there is another world, of massed engineers and design teams, but to him this is as the sound of lyres and flutes, of no more interest than the news bulletins which come on the hour and to which he listens like a bored, galactic emperor, in this small barn, once a blacksmith's forge. He is in a direct line of descent from the blacksmith, but nothing like him has existed before. The car underwrites the country. The Mechanic keeps the cars going until he finds himself welding air.

It took the Black Death to make the men of the late Middle Ages realise that everything in their world turned on the hunched figure out in the long fields, the labourer who produced the food, who until then they hadn't even noticed. Life is simpler now. It just takes the MOT. Yet writers on the country do not mention him, in whose garage we wait as humbly as our ancestors at a shrine, shuffling in case we stick to the floor, glumly reading 'Made in Japan' on a discarded box of plugs, staring at the girls.

'I used to book cars in on the calendars, wherever there was a space, and I wrote "Mrs Woods" once, only it was *where* I wrote it. Next thing is, Mrs Woods is staring at it and at me. Got a desk diary now.'

He reads no newspapers. The only news that interests him are the Ministry of Transport Directives which, amongst other things, mean he can no longer go out with a rope and tow cars off the motorway. He does not know what 90 per cent of his customers do for a living. All he knows is that from time to time they change their cars ('And, in your case, don't'). He does not frequent the village pub where men praise or revile him, discussing his bills with a passion that in towns they reserve for soccer stars. The Mechanic is the only public figure I know.

1998

Guardian of the Best of Times

PHIL LOOKS AFTER time for us. Religious faith made the men before him climb the steps to the church clock; Phil does so out of a sense of order, which may be the same thing in the end. 'I don't believe in God,' he reflected as we passed the brass of a fifteenth-century courtier, 'I believe in the human need for God.' He took the job on five years ago when, in his house on the hill above the church, he found he could no longer stand hearing the wrong hours being struck in the darkness below him. Phil is a scientist.

The trouble started in the 1950s when an electric motor was installed. Before that, above the steady clunk of the 12-foot pendulum, it had been necessary only to keep the clock wound. Afterwards, with every power cut, even those in the small hours which only villagers recording European pornographic films noticed, error sidled in like heresy from somewhere beyond the fields.

Phil has come to like his work, which above all has given him an excuse to visit the church. 'All those things being changed over the centuries, so much added.' He looked around him in genuine wonder. 'Bit like a privately-owned council house really.' He had invited me on a tour of the clock, adding, 'What are you like at heights?' The question surprised me, for the tower did not look that high. 'You'll be surprised,' said Phil, 'it's a bit odd up there.'

The church was extensively rebuilt in the 1890s, being the first of the new squire's priorities. Piped water came next, then the school, before the squire settled down to his ambition of solving the world's little mysteries, most of which lay beneath black bombazine skirts. What the rebuilding meant was that pillars and interior walls, even the gargoyles, are now of hard Victorian stone, except the little door to the side of the bellropes, which, like men on the frontier of fairyland, we crouched to enter. Beyond

66

that door is the thirteenth century. No hardness here, everything is blurred with use, and the winding narrow stair makes you think you are entering the heart of the stone. There is much white dust.

We emerged into a small empty room, with a long, long ladder leading up to the bells. About 15 feet up this, three planks had been laid across the beams to form a platform in front of the clock. The old pendulum, large enough to have interested Edgar Allan Poe, hung motionless. 'Shall I go first?'

I followed him up the ladder, watching with interest how he swung himself from it on to the platform. I inched my way after and stood there as he pointed out the Clerkenwell maker's name and the date, 1896; but with each movement the planks were quivering as though we were on a trampoline. Someone once described an earthquake to me and the terror of finding he could no longer brace himself against anything that did not move. It was like that on the platform and, feeling the steady onset of panic, I did what anyone would do in the circumstances: I began to ask intelligent questions. Unfortunately Phil, being of a scientific bent, felt obliged to answer these in full. He explained the blasted motor, the catching up with time, the replica dial on which everything moved anti-clockwise. And with each came a *practical* demonstration. Dear God.

That was when I asked if we might see the bells. 'Now?' he said. 'Yes,' I said. Poor, poor fool. We swung out again and climbed into a place of complete lunacy. Here *everything* moved. It is a cluttered place, of wood and metal and wheels, where if you steady yourself against a bell, it begins to roll. You move your grasp to one of the wooden stays and suddenly it is no longer there.

Somehow I got along the rafters to the window and clung to the slats. 'Shouldn't touch that,' said Phil, materialising at my side. 'Don't know how safe that is.' We looked down. 'You feel like a bird up here,' he said. 'You can see into all the gardens. Listen, you can hear people talking in the road.' And we could. At least I told him we could. 'Right, the roof next.' There was another ladder balanced on a beam. 'Things get a bit hairy now, but they won't bother you. Where are you? I say, that's the way down.'

I told Mr Brown the grocer about it. He had been up there when he was fifteen, when he hadn't been frightened of anything, and he had never been anywhere near them bells again. But old Phil, he had been like Quasimodo entering his kingdom.

1991

The Traveller

I AM STARING NOW at a headline in the world's most Thatcherite publication, the English-language *Moscow Business News*: 'Forget Pravda, Grab a helmet.' An agency in Russia now offers the entire uniform of the old Red Army, from underwear to peaked cap, at just over £7. Invoking the new god, Market Forces, the article brightly goes on to predict that grenade launchers will also soon be on sale in newspaper kiosks (for the man who has everything). Quantity, it claims, is unlimited.

But it isn't that which is so bizarre, it is the way in Middle England I got my hands on a 'free newspaper for people with choices'. A chap came into our village pub and handed it to me. Much-travelled Bob was back from another of his business trips.

A dusty, sunburnt man, he at first intrigued the regulars with his tales of distant places, then he made them restless, and finally he infuriated them. All villages in time acquire a traveller.

It was Douglas Blake who first called him Much-travelled Bob. 'There we'd be of an evening talking about normal things, like the survival of Mithraism in Wood End, then old Bob would start up about the cost of living in Jakarta. I mean, it's like having the news on all the time. Why, the other night Ken Vaughan . . . you know Ken Vaughan, chap that's converted the old charnel house and has dead monks calling on him like Avon ladies. Anyway, these monks are so regular in their habits – nice one, Blake – Ken's wondering whether they'll babysit for him. And there we were, having this serious conversation as to whether there was anything in the law to say why the dead shouldn't help around the house, when Bob starts telling us about the time he was hijacked and saw somebody shot in front of his eyes. We're not interested in stuff like that; it's unreal.'

The point is that Bob is part of a long tradition dating back to Sir John Mandeville, who in the Middle Ages wrote about men he had seen with heads growing below their shoulders. The traveller had arrived. I don't know whether you've noticed the number of pubs called The Saracen's Head strung out along the A5, but they must date back to the Crusades, the name a mocking reference to old soldiers who straggled back with improbable tales of massacre.

My father told me of such a man who had returned to Bancyfelin village with stories after the Boer War. 'Slip, slop, through the blood. Tread on something. Look down – your best friend's head. Terrible, terrible.' It was only much later they found out the fighting had been over before the man even reached Africa. Yet in that interval he had told them about snakes that put their tails in their mouths and bowled along like hoops, and of others so big and slow a man could sit on one and not be aware of its movement.

Much-travelled Bob doesn't tell stories like that; he talks about airport terminals and graft and ministerial kickbacks, yet still nobody believes a word he says. In villages the suspicion of travellers casts a long shadow. But then it is not in our interests to believe him. When you talk to someone about a cloudburst in Towcester and he tells you about monsoons in Sarawak, you dwindle; and no man likes to dwindle. Either you get restive and long to travel, like Ratty in *Wind in the Willows*, 'eager and light-hearted, with all the South in your face', or, like Mole, you close your mind to it.

We each have an inbuilt scale; in the origins of human language there were only three numerals – one, two and many – and to protect that scale we fit a lens-hood over the imagination. Travellers' tales are filed away under the numeral 'many', vague and improbable. So poor Bob jets in with more and more adventures for his stone-faced tribunal. 'Did you know you can hire a bodyguard for $3 a day in Moscow now?' he said. 'And for that the man provides his own gun.'

'That all?' sniffed Doug Blake. 'In Greens Norton he'd buy you a pizza as well.'

1993

Warden of the Paths

I HAVE JUST, gracefully and quietly, accepted public office, the first time I have done so since I was the absentee monitor at the Queen Elizabeth Boys' Grammar School, and, a judge in Israel, walked its corridors with a large book in which I wrote each morning the names of those who were not there. I am now the Warden of the Paths for this village.

This, now that the hereditary keepership of the Book of Armagh is no more, is probably the most romantic office to which a man may aspire. Beside it even the Warden of the Marches breathes compromise, for borders are arrived at through negotiation. But the Warden of the Paths is the keeper of the true way; my new office glitters with the metaphors of religion.

I was sworn in last week by Parish Clerk John Weekley in a private ceremony in which I was invested with the seals of office, a large map of the village and a pile of round, white metal discs with a black arrow upon them. I am uneasily aware of the mischief I can wreak with these discs. One, hammered at night into the Admiral's gatepost, could unleash the anoraked hordes onto his lawn the next time he hosts a Conservative garden party. I am become the destroyer of privacy and harvests. I could, of course, only do such a thing once, like those powers of the Queen that constitutional historians delight in describing. If these were ever exercised, they would be taken away, just like my little discs.

But the paths I guard are older than monarchy. Down them came the traders in flints, perhaps even the odd Phoenician wide-boy hawking dyes with his ears pricked for wolves in the thickets. These paths were old when the walking walls of Rome passed in the valley, and may even have been there before man tamed the horse. The first threat to their use was the hedge, when parson and squire conspired to cheat the poor of their rights to graze animals and walk freely, rights which had been theirs since Neolithic times. So I find myself the tribune of the people.

On their behalf I must see that no obstruction has been put across the paths, that when farmers plough them up (as they are entitled to), they must make good the surface within two weeks (at the risk of a £400 fine), see that the stiles are kept in repair and that there is no barbed wire. For these count as highways for legal purposes, and all roads were paths once. Some have even sunk back to being paths again, like the one I can see from my window, now just a ridge in a field after the rerouting of the road.

But on behalf of what people do I do this? Does the accountant in his BMW know that these footpaths even exist? Do the children, who once would have walked along them to school from the outlying hamlets? I doubt it. The last man thought to have used them to walk to work was a farm labourer called Ray Kelchur, and he did so because they represented a considerable short cut over the roads, between the Wars. Then the bicycle came and after that, the car.

The paths are of interest now only to the few eccentric villagers who prefer their dogs not to foul the playing fields, and to elderly strangers with maps who occasionally spring by. Apart from them, there is just the expedition organised perhaps once a decade by the parish council, when all those interested in walking the paths are invited to turn up; about ten do, who then slip and curse their way through undergrowth and mud. Curiously, the handful who do walk in the village tend to stick to the roads, one of them, a blonde, with a large stick as the result of a pressing invitation from a motorist.

But none of this matters. I remember commiserating with a canon in Lichfield Cathedral that an evensong should have been heard by only two people. 'My dear boy,' he said in surprise, 'you should come in winter with the snow on the ground and nobody here at all. Quite beautiful.' Similarly the paths exist, and I am their Warden.

I feel great ambitions stirring within me, for what were the great officers of state in their origin but the kings' valets? What was the chancellor but the man who looked after his chapel? And what if in a troubled time it should become generally known that somewhere there exists a just man, a Warden of the Paths?

With the red light of dawn behind him he paces the fields, wild creatures looking up without concern, for they see him so often. The path of the just is as the shining light. He wears the uniform of his office, an old cavalry cloak and a fur hat, a white metal disc with a black arrow on it hanging on his chest. He has applied to the College of Arms for suitable insignia. He . . .

Memo from John Weekley to the Parish Council: 'Somebody will have to talk pretty sharpish to the new Paths Warden . . .'

1995

The Last Villager

HE SAT UNDER A painting of a huge tropical sunset, his gallstone beside him in a honey jar. The gallstone was the size of a man's fist. He rattled the jar absently from time to time, the way a medieval churchman might have done with a casket containing holy bones to remind himself of some higher reality. He has lived all his life in the village and now most of his neighbours do not know him, just as he, who once knew the inhabitants of every house, does not know them. The Last Villager is old among strangers.

And stripped pine. And inglenooks. The inglenooks were bricked up in his father's time and now have been chipped out again. On his walks he passes immaculate houses called the Old Bakery, the Old Forge, the Old School; houses in which nothing moves after 7 a.m., for by then the commuters have gone. He has even begun to doubt his own memory of a time when these places were not immaculate, when men baked bread and shod horses in them, and there were children.

He used to enjoy reading the property columns of the local paper, chuckling over 'a magnificent stone-built property offering character accommodation', and puzzling as to whose cottage that had been. The prices were funny then, five years ago. £50,000. Now, with the M40 inching nearer every month, fantasy and estate agents have sealed off the village, like Brigadoon. £135,000. 'A rarely available one-bedroom flat in a prestigious listed building . . .' Listed building? That was the local workhouse. Almost every week a new 'For Sale' sign goes up and, now nearing eighty, he suspects that in old age he is among nomads.

He finds himself wondering what they do for a living, the young men in the company cars who come and go. Sixty years ago, when he was young, they would either have been on the land or down at the Hall. He was a gardener – 'a very capable, hard-working gardener, thoroughly reliable, willing and sober'. He folded the testimonial up and put it away in his wallet. His employer wrote that when he left for the War, so that it should impress the Germans.

He remembers when the roads were made, a steamroller crushing the stone, when electricity came and piped water. He was a choirboy when they buried the last Squire, 'and we followed the cortège to the grave-side and sang "Now the labourer's task is done"'.

He has seen the old village families drift away or get tidied up into the council houses, for there is no room in the new village for the names which appear for generation after generation in the churchyard. He unlocks his memories for the few people who seek him out, as they would once have sought out a survivor of Waterloo or Agincourt. Then he talks and talks and talks.

The village will survive him, but it will be a place where men will wonder why such a small village has tennis courts and a reading room where no one reads. They will stare at the coat of arms over the pub, the three billy-goat heads the Squire delicately chose for himself. They will be men walking through a film set.

1996

PART FOUR

THE SCHOOL

The Devil and the Schoolmaster

No PICTURE OF him exists. We do not know where he came from or what became of him. Like the gunfighter Shane, he appeared, and when his moment was over he had gone. Nobody would even have heard of him had not the village historian, turning page after page of spidery seventeenth-century calligraphy in the diocesan court records, come upon the Great Fight. There were no witnesses to this, and the man's opponent, whose sin was always pride, did not give evidence. All we have is the schoolmaster's own account of the six nights on the road above the village when he fought the Devil.

The village historian collects characters the way other men collect china. He has recorded reverently from his own childhood the butcher's reactions to the first radio. The man would bound out of his shop. 'Mine says it's going to rain. What does yours say?' He relayed the news. 'My Guy . . .' It was his usual oath. 'My Guy, this fianceer, know what 'e did? 'E stepped out of an airyplane over the Channel and drowned 'isself. And know what 'e had with him in the plane?' The old gentleman would stop at this point for dramatic effect. ''E had two short-horn typists.'

But the schoolmaster was something else. All the historian had to go on was the evidence to a seventeenth-century equivalent of an Industrial Tribunal. The village school had been founded in the fifteenth century by the lord of the manor before he came a cropper by choosing the wrong side at Bosworth, so because of that, and inflation, the schoolmaster was little better off than a labourer.

It was always an odd position. The schoolmaster was not a grandee like the rector; he was something lonely and in between: perhaps a disgraced graduate who had shuffled into the village, safe in the knowledge that roads were bad and news travelled slowly. With this man there were suggestions that he had known better days. Shocked villagers said they had heard him say, 'I care not for my patron or the school.' He had even, it was claimed, lost the keys to the school. And in an age when attendance was compulsory, he had not been seen in church in twelve months.

Then there was the boozing ('He hath often been seen lying drunk and, once, dead drunk'). But what counted most against him was his claim that on six nights he had fought the Devil, armed with a fork. This was 'mockery'. He lost his job, and another little bundle of rags blows out of recorded history. But there was one thing more – something which even now invests that grumpy drunk with supernatural grandeur.

You see, the schoolmaster never said he had beaten the Devil. What stops you in your tracks across 300 years is the modesty of his claim that he fought him to a draw.

1987

The Headmaster

ICAME ON NAME after familiar name, that of the squire who had
briskly signed his register and those of the boys whose backwardness had
been his despair, the names rising out of his faded handwriting into mon-
umental masonry. But I could not find the grave of the man who died in
this village 100 years ago.

It was his misfortune as headmaster to follow a paragon. In the School
Log he would have pored over the plaudits of Inspectors and that man's
masterful way with parents ('I shall be master of those I pretended to
govern'). You can feel his unease as he makes his own first entry: 'Children
rather listless and inattentive . . .' The unease was justified because in the
five terms that follow, a tragedy is played out in just forty pages. He came
with the spring and, unlike his predecessor, did not even introduce himself
by name; that was supplied by another hand when it was over. Mr
Wagstaffe came in 1891.

That the old School Logs have survived is unusual, but that they have
survived in the place where they were written, not in some archive, is
remarkable. The present headmaster found them in a shed, bound in oil
cloth and leather, when he took over twenty years ago. His entries in his
own log are circumspect and brief, as are those of his immediate predecessors. But 100 years ago Victorian heads, caught between grandees like
the squire and vicar and their own unwilling rural charges, opened their
lonely hearts in such books. These start in the 1870s with a chap called
Passmore, whom the oldest inhabitant, now ninety-two, remembers
because of a verse passed on through subsequent generations: 'Near the
green there stands a school / And in that school there is a stool / And on
that stool there sits a fool / Whose name is Billy Passmore.' He remembers
this because every generation interpolated the name of its own headmaster. Passmore's wild handwriting is out of another time, its blotted scrawl

indifferent to the indictments of HMIs and airily laconic ('Going on as usual'). In 1886 this stops abruptly and the paragon Pilkington has come, signing off in 1891 with details of a new, grander headship.

Wagstaffe's first job that summer term is to write out in full the Inspector's last daunting report on his predecessor ('This school is very well conducted . . .'). Still, things go well for the new head during the first week, until suddenly there is a cataclysm: an epidemic of measles closes the school down for a month. Then there is the harvest.

This seems to have taken him unawares, which suggests he was new to the country, where the harvest determined the length of the summer holidays. At the start of the winter term he writes: 'School opened after six weeks' holiday. Work as usual gone back very much.' That same month something he describes as 'the fever' strikes. 'We appear to be in for all the sicknesses imaginable in this village,' he records incredulously.

By December Wagstaffe is in despair. 'I am greatly tempted to resign my position as master of this school. I have had nothing but drawbacks since I came.' A few sentences further on there is the worried reflection, 'To attain the usual reports of the school in the face of such illnesses seems impossible.'

For rearing up over his small world was the Inspector's impending spring visit, and what made it worse was that on the eve of this, he himself went down with flu, and his wife took over the school. On his return he is even more obsessed: 'Arthur Welsh is very ill, indeed it is said he is dying. He will of course not be at the examination tomorrow.' That conclusion is hair-raising.

Two months later Wagstaffe is agonising over the fact that the results have still not come, so much so that when they do, it is an anticlimax. 'Was very pleased to hear we had done well again.' There are other compensations now, with the rarity of a boy called Emery whom he is coaching for a county scholarship. But when the excitement of Emery's success is over, Wagstaffe's one bleak comment is that he will miss his high-flyer.

His last outburst is over the school stove. The caretaker lit this at 8.25 a.m. in spite of his appeals that she should come in earlier; the first hour of school is impossible because of the smoke. In November he is taken ill, his temporary replacement entering in the Log that a new stove has arrived, and with it even more fumes.

But Wagstaffe was beyond all that now. The oldest inhabitant remembers a private grief that does not appear in these pages, the death of the headmaster's baby, and it was another hand which records that on 29 December, Wagstaffe himself died. I don't know his age, his first name or where he came from; I know nothing about him except that in this book you can reach out and touch a man who is passing by.

1992

The Perpetual Schoolboy

THE PHOTOGRAPH gives nothing away. I have been staring at the faces in an attempt to find something, an expression, the proximity of the eyes, a hidden sneer, anything which might explain the crimes. I know the crimes, having read the indictments over and over, and the names are seared into my memory. Walter Coleman . . . Alfred Bottoms . . .

'I remember old Alfie's wedding,' said Mr Reynolds. 'He could not afford a honeymoon, nobody round here could in them days. And that night, so he told the village the next day, when they went to bed his missus lay there and said, "Oh, Alf, I can't believe we're really married." "Jes' you wait till I get this other sock off," said Alfie.'

The photograph is, of course, a school photograph, and I have been scanning the faces and questioning men who might have known them as to what became of the bad boys from the School Log. When villainy is abruptly abandoned, mystery closes in. What became of the Sundance Kid? Come to that, what became of Harold Brown?

'Uncle Harold became a policeman,' said Mr Brown the grocer. 'Oh, he were a Tartar. Whenever they wanted someone to kick the card tables over, they called for him. Then one night he hit someone over the head with his truncheon and killed him. That were the end of Uncle Harold in the police.'

When you read the School Log, you enter a world of good and evil, of obsession and of retribution as righteous as any in the Old Testament. Dark figures jump out of the handwritten pages, and it is no use reminding yourself they were just schoolboys. To the man who kept the Log there was no perspective except that of the small world he shared with them. The stove smoked (the school stove always smoked) and the headmaster blinked through the fumes at evil incarnate.

And one name led all the rest. On 24 March 1890 the paragon Pilkington admitted into his big school a boy called Walter Coleman, who, he recorded incredulously, could not count to twenty. On looking into the matter he found the boy had made only fifty attendances the previous year; in a school where absence was frequent, with many of the pupils living in outlying hamlets, Pilkington had met the ultimate absentee.

Coleman, he wrote, refused to come unless brought by his mother and then, when she left, cried so loudly he upset the entire school. One April morning, after a month of this, Pilkington cracked and laid into Coleman with a cane, at which time, as though on cue, Mother Coleman appeared out of nowhere ('trespassing', noted the Head) and carried off her boy. Two days later the pair reappeared, but, refusing to apologise, were sent packing. Five days after this they were back again and somehow honour was satisfied ('After showing the woman her great mistake, I decided to have him back'). Pilkington did not mention Coleman for six months but then, briskly recording that the boy had been present only 93 times out of a possible 248, he tried to have him transferred to another school. Two days later he recorded his relief at having been able to pass the buck like Pilate. Only Coleman also came back.

Six months on he was again at the school, still bottom of whatever group of contemporaries he occasionally found himself among. In the end it was Pilkington who went, bequeathing his problem to his successor, who wrote, 'Coleman is again absent without any reason.' The headmaster Wagstaffe got the Attendance Officer, the dreaded whipper-in, to call on the family but was baffled when the man returned to say the boy had 'flu. Two months later Mrs Coleman was at the school with the certificate to show that her boy had gastric catarrh. He was ten and had never got beyond Standard One.

Wagstaffe died, and his successor Dobedoe wrote that Coleman was again away ill. Six months later there was a glimpse of poverty when his mother called to say he was at home as he had no boots fit to wear to school. Dobedoe made no comment, but when Mrs Coleman – whose attendance record must have been better than her son's – called to say that another boy had hit him on the head, recorded that he must have deserved this. By then Walter was old enough to work in the fields, and the words 'illegally employed' accounted for the odd absence, though the magnificent march past of illness continued, sore throats giving way to toothache.

Our last glimpse of him is extraordinary, for at the end it was *Coleman gloriosus*. In March 1895 the Inspector called, and five boys, recorded Dobedoe proudly, made no mistakes at all in their papers. Among the names is an incredible one: Walter Coleman, Standard One. Strange the head should have forgotten to mention that by then Walter had been five years in Standard One. It was his last exam and he had come top. With that he disappears from the School Log, too long ago even for the oldest inhabitant to remember, but it is not easy to forget Walter Coleman in his pomp.

1993

A School Buried in Bumf

THEY WERE OFTEN in a state of siege, his predecessors. The handwriting in the School Log records their fears: the bad weather which, with no school bus, could empty a classroom, the epidemics of measles and of a mysterious thing called 'the itch' which could close the whole school down; and that Nemesis which came with every spring, the HMI. But the present village headmaster is the first of them to fear the postman.

'We had a whole parcel on Aids the other day. I think one of the staff used that to back pictures.' A thin man in a knitted cardigan, he sat in his office surrounded by forms and boxes and ring-bound files; a colleague, he said, had talked of suffocation by ringbinders. 'The stuff just keeps coming by every post.'

Twenty years ago, when he took over, his post had its excitements: a circular from County Hall perhaps once a month, a mother's request that her child might be excused netball, notice that the dentist was coming. Not now. A school of 100 pupils is now the main stop on the village postman's round; between ten and twenty letters a day come, some of them, said the head apprehensively, addressed to him as Chief Executive.

'My most pressing problem is not the National Curriculum or the new tests, it is the actual storage of paper.' The noticeboard behind his desk has just one thing on it, printed in large heart-felt capitals: 'Anyone who isn't confused doesn't really understand what is going on.'

Statutory instruments from the DES. The headmaster lives in a world of acronyms now, to which five years ago the LEA helpfully sent a large index, the way a spymaster equips his agents with a code book. This starts with AACDT (Association of Advisers in Craft, Design and Technology) and ends in YWS (Young Workers' Scheme). 'Bless them, they meant well but the things have doubled since then.'

After one awed glimpse, suddenly fearful for his sanity, he now files the statutory instructions unread ('In these Regulations, unless the context otherwise requires, any reference to a numbered regulation is a reference to the regulation bearing that number in these Regulations . . .'), just as he files the Department's circulars and its administrative memoranda. He was once a neat man, he said wistfully. Animals and Plants in Schools. 'Animals are not found in schools as often as they could be . . .' Fair enough, but there is more. '*All members of the crocodile and alligator family . . . have no place in schools.*'

On his shelves sits the National Curriculum, four full sets of which are in the classrooms of this small school, the reports of its working parties becoming the proposals of a Secretary of State before swelling into the diapason of the curriculum's stately volumes, each one the size of a family Bible.

Conscious he is living through a moment of history, the headmaster has begun taking his own photographs. He arranged his weekly post on two tables to record this for his governors, and when the papers for the new tests for seven-year-olds came, he had a child pose beside them: the parcel was one third her size. Eleven children in the school are taking this test.

Then there is the junk mail. 'Letters from insurance companies, from computer salesmen and photocopying firms, people who offer management training and advice on personnel problems or who want to sell books on this or that. Everyone's so helpful suddenly.'

Yet once his was the loneliest job in the world. You get a glimpse of what he was up against in Flora Thompson's *Lark Rise*, the real-life village being just 12 miles away. 'If the children by the time they left school could read well enough to read the newspaper and perhaps an occasional book for amusement, and write well enough to write their own letters, they had no wish to go further. Their interests were not in books, but in life, and especially in the life that lay immediately about them. At school they worked unwillingly, upon compulsion, and the life of the headmistress was a hard one.'

In the School Logs you read of their despair, for 100 years ago men opened their hearts in such books. Not about the curriculum – there were no doubts then about the curriculum – but without immunisation there were the epidemics ('We appeared to be in for all the sicknesses imaginable in this village'), the absences ('Anything unusual like the killing of a pig could empty the school, so in the end the head just allowed them all out when the Hunt came'), and the damning report of an HMI ('We have failed utterly . . .').

In living memory, entries in the School Log are circumspect. In the present head's one-line reports it is only references to increased staff meetings and to new training courses that alert you to the fact that the National Curriculum has come. With so many now looking over his shoulder, a man grows careful.

The headmaster is not opposed to the Curriculum, in fact he welcomed its coming. 'In the 1960s I was on a term's secondment, and we were taken to see a school. We didn't stumble on it, this was a showpiece. A new head had been appointed and he'd pulled down all the interior walls so there were children everywhere. They'd been given tasks to do but so far as I could see, most were doing bugger all. They called the teachers by their Christian names. I don't think I was horrified, more worried it might become the norm, for I knew I couldn't have operated like that.

'Yet in the 1980s I was taken to a large primary school to see a building conversion. It was mid-morning, we were there an hour, and in that time I didn't see – or hear – a single child. Now there were several hundred children in that school but it was like walking round a hospital with no patients in it. Each of these is an extreme case, and those who were with me recognised them as such. For whatever you read in the papers, most schools didn't change that much; they steered a middle course. Which is why someone like myself who had gone on teaching the three Rs welcomed the National Curriculum. It gave me a lot of confidence.'

I looked over the heap of files and circulars. 'Until the postman called?'

'Until the postman called,' he said mildly.

School was over for the day, the cleaners were in and their cupboard stood open. 'Just look at this.' Among the mops and spare bulbs there was a whole shelf given over to ring-bound files. The headmaster pulled one of these out, a thing the size of an atlas entitled Safety Data Sheets. It had an unread look. Every product was there, from Brasso to Windolene, its chemical constituents analysed, its hazards listed. I opened this at random and began to read. '*Ink . . . no protection against this is needed when it is in the pen.*'

None of this is fantasy.

1995

The Spare Knickers Drawer Closes

TIME IS SUDDENLY confusing. She hears the children's voices, but the play-times, which for thirty years were over almost as soon as they had begun, now seem to last forever. In her cottage across the green from the village school, the infants teacher is in the first month of her retirement.

You cannot forget your infants teacher however hard you try, and you did try. For some teachers you loathed, some you loved, but there was one over whom you can still feel guilt. Remember how, at seven, you were as dismissive of your infants teacher as any Tory MP is of his uncertain social origins? But then she had seen you in your beginnings, before you assembled the mask that got you through school. She saw you that first morning when your mother had gone. She picked you up when you fell, comforted you when you cried, helped conceal the shameful little accidents. And how quickly you betrayed her, mocking the sand and the Bible stories, sneering with your peers in the corner of the playground. Remember?

The Infants is the oldest wing of the school, so old not a single word is legible in the plaque above the long window. Once it housed the whole school, and when she came thirty years ago the stove was still there over which successive Victorian masters muttered. It fumed then, as it had always fumed, and over this she can remember the smell of wet socks and gloves drying.

She is not sure why she became an infants teacher. One girl at training college, whose ambition this was, changed her mind abruptly at her first teaching practice when she saw the drawer marked 'Spare Knickers'. It had been a college with all the bright dogma of the 1960s. Children should not be taught to read until they were ready to read. Children should explore. She retires amid the jargon of the National Curriculum, with its base-line assessments and Key Stage One. The infants teacher has lived through more educational change than anyone since the Reformation.

Children have changed. At the end they came to her after years of expensive toys and television, so over-stimulated they had lost the ability to play. She saw them start to amble round the playground like lifers in a prison yard. She also saw parents change. Once they had surrendered their children to the school, but now they were older and difficult to cope with, being so very helpful.

Some change she was shielded from, for it was a village school. In towns she would have become used to being kicked and sworn at; as it is, she remembers the shock of hearing a child aged five use the F word. But such things were rare. An infants teacher, she said, even now had more absolute authority than anyone else in the school. It had allowed her to ignore certain directives. She immediately put away the plastic gloves which came with instructions that they had to be worn whenever a child fell over and there was blood that might 'contaminate'.

In other schools the children disappeared afterwards. In a village she saw them grow up, and most, she said, turned out the way she thought they would. In the faces of small boys the self-importance or the confusion was already there at five, some of them having been born looking forty. What was sad was spotting those who stood no chance. But in one respect nobody changed. They still loved stories, though the fashions changed. What made her feel as old as the hills was when, nearing retirement, she found herself having to explain who Jesus Christ was.

The best thing that happened in her career was an end to that harrowing first day at school. She can still remember children being dragged from their mothers, but with nursery schools and regular visits all that had gone. But the old freedom had gone with it, when she could say, 'What shall we do today, boys?' There was a policy on everything now, the shadow of the Ofsted inspection falling on the sand and stories. That she had made it into her sixties was a source of wonder to her. Her colleagues had all gone in their fifties.

Throughout her time at the school a relic of the old world hung outside her room: a bell that in living memory no one had heard ring. But at her leaving party a former pupil, who heard her say this, went home for a ladder. And she, seeing him climb this to attach a rope, spread cushions at the ladder's foot, for old habits die hard. Later she realised that the first time she heard the bell ring, it was a knell for her own career.

1998

PART FIVE

THE CHURCH

Vicars

I

FREDERICK HUGGINS, licensee of the New Inn at Abthorpe in Northants and as temperate a man as only a retired Sergeant Major can be, was pacing up and down the bar of his pub like a caged beast. Up and down, up and down. 'Well, what would you do?' he appealed to Young Gascoigne, the famous collector of militaria.

'Do what, Fred?' said Young Gascoigne, startled out of one of his humbler daydreams in which, in a Panzer Tiger, he was leading a VE parade down the Mall.

'About what's been appearing in the papers about our church?'

'Just thank God I don't go to church.'

But Fred does, and as church warden, he is closely involved in the efforts of the three joint parishes of Abthorpe, Silverstone and Slapton to find a new vicar. He has thus taken personally, these past two weeks, the sudden bizarre interest of a national newspaper in this. 'It's the fantasy I can't take. They said we're advertising for a vicar in *The Spectator*, *The Field* and in *Motoring Life*, a magazine that doesn't even exist. We're advertising in *Auto-sport*. Also in *Motorcycling News*,' said Fred, indignantly. 'Of course, we're in *The Church Times*, too, but there's Silverstone to consider, as well as the other two parishes.'

It is with some trepidation that I again involve myself in the affairs of Slapton church, that tiny medieval jewel where two years ago they raised the Devil. A wild horned figure, he appeared from behind the whitewash of centuries, and the congregation of nine then had to find £10,000 to preserve the wall painting. I wrote about this and about the efforts of the late David Mumford, a lovely man, who was the church warden, to raise this. Mumford approached the Historic Churches Preservation

Trust, which to his surprise said its brief did not cover wall paintings. The Devil then entered into one of us (which one was a matter of some dispute), for when the story appeared, the Historic Churches Preservation Trust was quoted as saying that it was 'not in the business of preserving historic churches'. At which point the roof duly fell in on the two of us, and I subsequently wrote the most factual article I have ever written, describing the Trust's laudable work in many English churches in some detail.

'I remember that,' said Fred Huggins. 'It was almost as bad as the time you wrote about me and called me Huggett all through the article, and you'd been coming here for years.'

'Or when you described me taking my driving test in a tank,' said Young Gascoigne.

'But you did.'

'Yes, I did.' And he settled back to a daydream in which, dressed in the uniform of a colonel in the Brunswickian Death's Head Hussars, he reviewed the Women's Institute.

The local living has been vacant since the tragic death of the vicar, Jack Smith, a Falstaffian man with a liking for Carlsberg Special. This meant that Fred saw a lot of him in his dual capacity as church warden and licensee. The Revd Jack Smith had ministered to all three churches, in each of which he conducted a different form of service. 'That's what gave me most grief in the newspaper articles,' said Fred. 'They said we were look-ing for a man to hold the 1662 Service, but that's just Slapton. In Silverstone they hold Rite A, and in Abthorpe, Rite B.'

'So you're worried you're going to get a whole lot of chaps in lace turn-ing up, hoping to do the 1662?'

'I thought that was a Kronenbourg lager,' said Young Gascoigne, but nobody was listening to him.

'And what's worse,' said Fred, 'some London businessman thinks he's the Patron and tells the paper he wouldn't mind a woman vicar – "gel who could ride side-saddle with the Grafton".'

'You'd really have a shock if a woman got the job,' said Young Gascoigne.

'No, we wouldn't, there's a lot of them out there,' said Fred. 'And you'd get a lot of work out of a woman.'

And he should know, he who was once the most sought-after bachelor in England. Holed up in a Falklands farmhouse, Fred found an old newspaper crossword and sent this in, six years late, explaining the circumstances. The paper printed the story, so when the war was over, and the mail came, a soldier struggled up to their position with two sacks, one small, one enormous. 'Little one's for the Regiment,' he muttered. 'Big bugger's yours.'

Young Gascoigne gave what Barbara Cartland might call a mocking laugh, and strode out into a night where we could hear the motorcycle escort starting up in the cloisters of his mind.

II

A NEW PARSON has been appointed to the village. The processes of the Church of England, as convoluted as any which produce the Dalai Lama, are in their final stages, and in faraway Guernsey a man weary of tax-dodgers and tomatoes has heeded the call. He comes in the spring.

We have now been without a parson for six months, ever since the incumbent departed – joyfully – because he had never liked the country. Thirty years ago, even twenty, such events would have been a matter of public interest, and the further back you go, the more anxious the public would have been. Now parsons come and go and I doubt half the inhabitants even know their names.

So what will he be coming to? A brisk, little, modern house – for, like most villages, we have an Old Rectory now, the Church having cashed in on rural property prices. But the new parson will also be coming to a building inside which the names of his predecessors go back in an unbroken line to the thirteenth century, a locked building to which he will have the key. Only the oldest inhabitants can remember a time when the door was left open; soon only they will remember when the eighteenth-century tombstones with the recurring cherub faces were not stacked in a mean-ingless line against the graveyard wall.

But hold the key in your hand for a moment. It is 10 inches long, shiny with use and heavy enough to be a weapon, a key for castle keeps or dun-geons. Passed from generation to generation, it may itself be hundreds of years old, for long before a Chubb or Banham interested himself in such things, this key turned in this lock. Yet it takes an extraordinary event for you to appreciate the fact. Not that long ago, the police raided a house about 15 miles away and found the walls festooned with church keys; the man had been stealing them for years. But this was not one of them, so come inside, past the noticeboard which reveals that the summer fête raised £710.06, to which my copy of the book *History of Orgies* contributed (I bought it back).

Now there is the smell you get nowhere else, the mustiness of old mats, some damp, and the faint aroma of polish. Not a church for con-noisseurs, this; a hundred or so years ago, Daddy Bigbucks lived at the Hall, so the church has the anonymity of a late Victorian facelift. The gar-goyles are hard and sanitised. Which is why in the visitors' book the names of the past three years occupy just three-quarters of just one page, and there is no eccentricity, except for a schoolboy who gives his nationality as 'pan-galactic'.

No stained glass in the nave, so the light is bleak too. Perhaps they never could afford it, or perhaps that industrious Puritan 'Smasher' Dowsing called and broke the lot, charging 6/8d a church as he always did. And it is easy to forget what this place was, that once men were prepared to kill each other over interior decoration.

See those rails around the communion table? Archbishop Laud's insis-tence on those set in train the events which led to the Civil War and his own execution. The irony is that the little red-faced meddling man still had his way; you have only to note the nagging awe in yourself when you come in here. Laud inherited a Church in which, in Wales, men shot birds in the nave, and, in Essex of course, a woman hung up her washing in the chancel, saying that if the parson could bring his old linen in, so could she. Look around you: this was a battlefield. Yet something was lost with Laud, for never again could a church have its old casual medieval youth; nobody in the village now would think of holding a public meeting here. Neglected or not, this is a special place.

The authority Laud insisted on has also gone. You find yourself grinning at the notice listing the thirty categories of people you may not marry. 'A Man May Not Marry His Grandmother' . . . as though England once boiled with men who wanted to do so. 'His wife's father's sister . . .' Who is she? And why ever not? Then there is the rest of it: the old crib produced year after year, the jumble of vases in a corner, a toy lamb, a warning to bell-ringers ('we are unable to guarantee the safety of the bells'), the names of the almost-forgotten dead in two world wars. Just another church.

To which a man is now coming. I wish him well, for what he faces here will dwarf anything encountered by his listed predecessors: the fact that people pass by.

III

IT WAS SUCH a beautiful morning. I filled my pipe slowly, playing for time and the inspired reason which would allow me to put off work. From my window I could see the dull gleam of keys where they hung in the Reverend Comberpatch's open door, and, below me, the post lady in our drive. She was moving, I noticed, much faster than usual.

A weekday village is an eerie place in the late twentieth century. In the early morning the fathers have all gone, at 9 a.m. the cars swarm briefly around the school, and then there is an empty time. A coal lorry calls, a black cat crosses a green field, and at a typewriter a man dreams of an argumentative Jehovah's Witness to brighten his day. I started, for the post lady was knocking loudly on my door.

She was worried. At seven, when she had gone to work, the vicar's door was open; three hours later it was still open. Now the vicar, a bachelor and punctilious man, is a former prison chaplain; he never leaves doors open. What was worse, he had been due to go on holiday the day before.

We paused at the front door, nervous of what we might find. I pushed the inner door open but the hall was as immaculate as ever. In the study I came on part of the Gothic cathedral the vicar has been building out of matchsticks for forty years, which is so vast the nave alone fills the room. There was no sign of violence anywhere. But then, as we entered the kitchen, that insistent film music that turns the screws on terror, what my daughter calls the 'dan-dan-dans', started in my head. On the table was a half-empty pint of milk and some boiled ham wrapped in cellophane. We were in *Marie-Celeste* territory. After a fortnight's absence a man would find such things crawling to greet him on his return, so whoever left the house last had clearly been in a terrible rush.

The tension was increasing, for a neighbour remembered seeing the door open the night before. We rang the Bishop, who, it turned out, was also on holiday. We rang the Archdeacon, who said he could name eighteen vicars quite capable of such behaviour, but not the Revd Comberpatch. This was completely out of character. So where had he gone? One of his parishioners thought the vicar was staying with a brother in Hastings. I rang directory enquiries who confirmed there was a Comberpatch in Hastings, but he was ex-directory. What was more, he was in a category which did not even accept calls from the operator.

I got the supervisor and told her this was an emergency. She advised me to ring the Hastings police, which I did. The station sergeant was apologetic but said there was nothing they could do; it was now British Telecom policy not even to give the police the address of an ex-directory subscriber. Dear God.

The Archdeacon rang. The Archdeacon was to ring many times. He said he was getting more alarmed the more he thought about it and asked, did I have the vicar's car number? I rang the village garage office. By now the morning had gone. I looked down and saw the church warden had come to look over the house. The cast list was increasing.

By early afternoon it had increased considerably. The Archdeacon called again, saying he had located his Hastings counterpart who, it turned out, had the chief executive of the local council as a parishioner. The chief executive had personally checked the council computer and said there was no

Comberpatch listed for Hastings. Of course, he might have neglected to register for the poll tax. Oh, calamity, as the old actor Robertson Hare used to say. The Archdeacon, now choosing his words with care, said he did not know how far to go on this one.

At 5 p.m., having come to the conclusion that my day was a write-off, I heard the post lady shouting up from the lane. The vicar had been found. Phil, who looks after the clock and is currently trying to stop it slowing, had called for the tower keys just before the vicar left. He had been going not to Hastings, but to his other brother, a schoolmaster in Suffolk. Phil had rung the school and the vicar was there.

The vicar rang in the evening, a worried man who wondered aloud whether he was going mad, leaving his door open and the keys in the lock. But not half so mad as he will be when he gets home and finds that not only have I been giving guided tours of his house, I have also shopped his brother as a poll-tax rebel. Two days later I met the post lady. That morning, she said, she had found the back door of one of the retirement bungalows wide open, and she burst out laughing. I did not laugh.

1994

The Church in the Fields

W HEN I FIRST saw the church in the fields, I found the sight so
beautiful and so mysterious it was as if *Le Morte D'Arthur* had come
to life. There was no village near and no road leading to it. And the church
was old. Inside, there were the tombs of men in armour and the small
stained glass of the Middle Ages: everything seemed a pointer to a purer,
forgotten faith. I did not know then that the beauty was peripheral. What
this was about was tragedy, a very old tragedy. The church in the fields was
a pointer all right, but what it pointed to was not a forgotten faith, but a
forgotten crime.

The church is by a lake in the park of the stately home called Fawsley,
and what follows is its story and that of another church at Charwelton.
Both are near Daventry in that south-eastern corner of Northamptonshire
where it borders Oxfordshire, and are within five miles of each other. You
will find it easy to locate Charwelton, for the village is on the main
Daventry to Banbury road, though you will not find the church there. Just
as at Fawsley, it is out in the fields and, again, contains tombs of men in
armour.

Treat this as a mystery tale. Ask yourself who builds English churches
out in the fields. The answer has to be that nobody does. So look around
you at those fields and at sunset you will see shadows in the grass and an
uneven surface. This is the first clue. Now step inside the church at
Fawsley, through the tiny door set deep in the medieval stone. Tombs
occupy two-thirds of the church and one of them an entire wall, so that
whoever preached here did so across the dead to a small cluster of the
living. And the dead are very grand: they lie in alabaster and brass, and
from their armour they appear to have been members of a knightly caste.

The irony is that although their name was Knightley, probably not one
of them ever went to war, yet here they lie in armour, very perfect gentle

knights, which is how they wanted to be remembered. The tombs are not quite so grand at Charwelton, though they too date from the late Middle Ages and belong to a family called Andrew. These men were more honest about their origins.

If you pull back the matting in the aisle, which is about the length between the creases of a cricket pitch, you will find three brasses flush with the floor. The first commemorates a man who died in 1497, when Henry VII was king, and is shown in a long gown. Clearly the founder of the family fortunes, he is described as 'Mercator', a merchant. By the second brass the gown has gone and the man's son is in armour; he is described as 'Generosus', gentleman. His son, also in armour, is described as 'Armiger', esquire. The pace of social mobility is accelerating and the merchant's great-grandson does not lie under the floor at all but is much nearer the altar and in three-dimensional alabaster. He is 'Miles', a knight, and a sculpted lion lies at his feet, for the process is complete: the Andrew family has become part of chivalry, its humble origins erased.

So how did this come about? To find out you must start again at the first funeral brass, for it is not quite true to say that the Andrew family wanted entirely to erase their origins. There was a small streak of humility in them. They may not have wanted to proclaim the reason for their social rise, but they did want it recorded, so under the merchant's foot is the foundation on which all the grandeur and the alabaster rested. It is the figure of a tiny sheep chewing a sprig of clover. And this is your second clue.

The Andrew family and the Knightleys have both long gone but the sheep remain, grazing among the bumps in the field. Only once these weren't fields. The shadows show where lost streets were, the bumps the houses that stood along them when there were villages here, before the men from those two families who lie in armour closed them down, demolishing the houses and evicting the inhabitants to make way for sheep. They were farmers who became rich.

You will have heard of the sheep clearances in the Scottish Highlands in the early nineteenth century because men recorded the agonies of whole communities broken up, forced to emigrate or starve, the land given over to pasture. Years later, at the time of the Crimean War, the main culprit, the Duke of Sutherland, was trying to recruit men for battle as Highland chieftains had always done. One man told him, 'Send your sheep to fight the Russians.'

But the events that left the churches in the fields happened too long ago for there to have been any sort of organised protest. These were small agonies to which the few men recording historical events were indifferent. All we hear is the odd murmur. 'Where forty persons had their livings, now one man and his shepherd have all,' Bishop Latimer said in a sermon before King Edward VI. The people themselves were more direct: 'Sheep do eat up men.'

In the Middle Ages sheep represented the fastest shortcut to great wealth, for English wool and English cloth clothed Europe, and by the end of the fifteenth century, merchants such as Andrew of Charwelton were getting in on the act. But as they turned themselves into country gentlemen, they brought a new ruthlessness. In just fifteen years, from 1485 to 1500, 13,000 acres in the Midland counties became vast sheep ranches.

This alarmed even the Crown, for suddenly there was a flood of vagrants in Middle England, little homeless groups of children and their parents roaming the countryside, unwanted in the towns and a potential source of disorder. But there was little the Crown could do, for the men who sat in Parliament and were justices of the peace were the men responsible for the evictions. They had done well out of the dissolution of the monasteries, one of the Knightleys of Fawsley being among the lawyers sent out to confiscate the property of the monks. This man was actually prosecuted for closing the village of Snorscomb four miles to the east of Fawsley, one of the rare prosecutions, and was found guilty, but the fine was a trifle. At the crossroads today a sign still points to the village, though there is no Snorscomb and hasn't been for 500 years.

Neither is there a Fawsley, once one of the largest Northamptonshire villages (the poll tax of 1377 records ninety taxpayers), formerly a Saxon town and centre of justice. In the nineteenth century the Northamptonshire gazetteer records with some puzzlement: 'There is no village in this parish.' But it did not go on to speculate over why this should be. In the guide to Charwelton church a former vicar did try. Most probably this had something to do with the Black Death, he said, which is the reason people generally give to account for a lost village, as though England had infinite land resources. He did not mention the clearances.

What happened to those who once worshipped in those churches and were thrown out on to the roads? Nobody knows. But just to give you an idea of the upheaval there must have been in their lives, remember that not long before, they would have needed the permission of the lord of the manor just to move outside the village. And the men who did this? The Andrew family and Knightleys are gone, but the biggest sheep farmers are still at Althorp and have no need to enquire why there should be a church in the fields, so beautiful, so mysterious.

1993

Here He Stands, He Can Do No Other

IAM HOLDING a piece of wood, only I have never seen wood like this before. It is so light, if I throw it into the air it might float. If I close my hand on it, this honeycomb might crumble into dust. Yet this was oak and until a few weeks ago, part of the church roof. People sat under this. I met the carpenters, affable men, at ease with the world, for they know their place in it as the last master-craftsmen, who replaced the wood and stretched a new roof of lead over it; it was the biggest repair to the church in a century.

For it was exactly 100 years ago, almost to the day, that the last squire paid for a rebuilt chancel. The village band played, everyone praised the squire, and even the Bishop came, who made a little speech and said he feared he would soon be like the Bishop who could open everything except his own umbrella. They all had lunch at the Hall, and it was a day of marquees and congratulation, which they must have thought would go on forever.

Only the Hall has long ago been pulled down, there is no squire or village band, and when the present Vicar tried to get some dignitary of his church to officiate at the centenary, he found no one was available. But the new roof is up and the church stands. I am walking round it with the Vicar, who after five years is having to get used to the outrageous luxury of not being rained on as he preaches.

It is not a beautiful church, and nobody writes 'a little gem' in a visitors' book: just another church in an English village. Yet, as I follow the Vicar, I am struck again by what an extraordinary place this is. When it was built in stone, its congregation lived in a world of wood and mud. Victorians took away its plaster (and who knows what paintings that hid?), but I can still see in the stonework the outline of a sharply pitched roof that would have been thatched and old when the tower was added in the reign of Edward I.

At the altar rails there is a strange little moment as I hang back and ask the Vicar if he minds my accompanying him into an area where traditionally only the priest and his attendants went. 'I might grumble if you had a cigarette in your mouth,' murmurs the Vicar. But then his own position has changed. Once, as he says, he would have stood here, God's representative on earth. Now he is just the people's chairman, and that is a momentous change.

I do not attend this church, but, even though I am the Vicar's closest neighbour, this absence is one thing we do not discuss. His predecessor called after my daughter was born, and made small talk over a long, long tea. It was only later we guessed he had found himself unable to bring up the matter of her christening. But the church stands.

And, whether we attend it or no, each of us in the village thinks of it as his, just as the English Heritage people think of it as theirs. The letters come and go, discussing damp and building materials. Committees meet. Accountants submit figures. It is very easy to forget that this is also one man's place of work.

The Vicar does not like the Victorian restoration. It may have added 14 feet to the chancel and allowed him to officiate from behind the altar, instead of hovering to one side, but a pillar hides his stall from the congregation, so for much of the service he is a disembodied voice. The Vicar is considering coming out of the chancel altogether, as he has already done in one of his churches. For he has four, which would have made him a pluralist on a scale beyond the dreams of his predecessors. Just as in the dying Roman Empire, a man's position becomes grander on paper as his power wanes.

He locks the door with the usual enormous key, and the massed chimneys of the old rectory loom over us, long ago sold off by the Church. 'If I had my way, I'd hand all these places over to the Ancient Monuments,' he says suddenly. 'But they're there and we are stuck with them.'

As we walk down the path, he impishly directs my attention to a sign he has had put up, 'Danger. Slippery Path', and it occurs to me that I am in the company of one of the loneliest men on earth. For the church stands.

1998

A Cycle of Chapels

I: Prehistory

JUST BEFORE NOON we passed a party of young men moving north. I asked the one with a map where they had come from and he pointed behind him to the line of trees on the horizon. They were not communicative men. There were ten of them, and I had seen them coming from some distance away, dressed in the bits and pieces of disbanded armies. Out here a man is nervous of such meetings. But then they were gone, one of them singing, his voice quickly lost in the wind.

It was a sly wind. Among the trees we had not even noticed it but now, on the earth's shoulder, it leapt upon us, boxing the compass and making a mockery of the winter sunlight. My wife and I walked with our heads down, our small daughter grumbling. There were white bones underfoot, the skulls and ribcages of sheep, as we stared down into a hollow lined with trees and vegetation, with the sound of water far below. In such a place the monster Grendel from the Anglo-Saxon epic *Beowulf* might have lurked, and even my daughter, who is proof against mythology, stopped grumbling when I told her that in another climate this might have concealed an anaconda.

There were traces of man all round us in that hollow, the rusted remains of a windpump from which the sails had gone but the brick shaft of which still went neatly into the earth, and looking down I could see machinery far below me in the water. Someone at some point had clearly gone to a great deal of trouble to have this built, so why abandon it? But then out here so many things had been abandoned.

Before us, our journey's end, was a house around which a religious community once turned, far from the eyes of plump vicars and the King's hard-faced magistracy, carrying out its baptisms in secret here. The roof of the house has fallen in and the whole structure is slowly settling into the earth, the last door being already below ground level so it looks like the entrance to a bunker. The elder tree holds illimitable dominion.

The house looks centuries old but ruin must have come quickly and in our time, for outside there was a rusting hayrake of the sort I remember my cousin using on his farm, riding that line of sabres and moving the handle to send them hissing into the grass.

The pool itself can still just be seen – even in winter with the trees thick around it – but you can make out the broken bricks where they gathered, their hems ragged in the wind, as one of their number caught his breath below them in the water. For this they were prepared to defy Church and State.

What made it so poignant for me was that I myself am a backslider from these rites, and went through such ceremony at my mother's insistence ('Why do you have to be different?'). By then they had come in from the fields, and the pool was in the chapel pulpit where, wadered and in a black gown, the minister waited. The girls went first, all of them in filmy white which, as they climbed out of the pool, became totally diaphanous. I pressed my face into my hands and groaned aloud, for I was sixteen years old.

Could there have been someone like me under the trees? I doubt it. These were the children of men who in the open day had killed their king and so were obliged to meet here in secret to celebrate their faith. I felt humble in that place.

The return journey was a sort of time travel, for where we had been was just a mile or so from the road, yet we had heard no cars all morning and, apart from the walkers, had met no one. We crossed three fields and 300 years to emerge in 1994 in Northamptonshire.

II: The Great Preacher Comes

FOR TEN YEARS I had passed the chapel without a glance. They are so self-effacing, these little chapels of Middle England, and had to be when squire and parson opposed their building. What made me stop was a sentence from a volume of nineteenth-century reminiscence: '*Had he not feared God he would have been terrible, for he feared no man.*' I was in search of the great preacher.

In the 1950s I still believed in such a man. There was a serial on *Children's Hour* called 'The Face in the Rock', about a small boy's quest for the hero whose profile is that formed in the rock of the mountain above his valley. He seeks for him in the great politician, poet, preacher, soldier, the remarkable thing being that the great preacher was then considered hero material. How odd that seems now.

I heard the last of them, being taken by my father to hear Martin Lloyd Jones, also in the 1950s. I remember people's faces afterwards, their eyes shining, and a matron in the balcony lifting her left breast to indicate to a friend the effect of the sermon. These were not the apologetic ten-minute sermons of the Established Church: they lasted an hour and more, and the men who delivered them were as famous as pop stars – particularly in the late nineteenth century, when Spurgeon attracted congregations of 3000, one of his published sermons selling 300,000 copies. And where are the great preachers now?

The village of Kilsby is a mile from Rugby, though you would not know that from the road signs which hustle you on towards the A5 and the M1. The road past the chapel has also been twitched away, for this now stands among modern houses in its own layby of dissent. It is more like a house than a chapel, but inside there is the old smell compounded of pine, damp and windows that are never open. No impediments of humankind here, no carving, just a bleak room cleared for action around the pulpit where in the 1840s he stood, Kilsby Jones, the great preacher.

I have sat in judges' chairs, on bishops' thrones and once, on a quiet afternoon, on the Throne of England, but not one of them gave the feeling of power that is in the pulpit of this small non-conformist chapel. There a man stood between heaven and earth.

His name was James Jones, a farmer's son from Llandovery, who took the name Kilsby after his first ministry here. He looked amazing, being well over 6 feet, with a high forehead and long white hair and a trifurcated beard worn low on his chest. He also carried a shepherd's crook 7 feet high. But his contemporaries could have coped with that. What stunned them was that in an age of sanctimoniousness this man mocked Hell-fire sermons ('Men saying there were babies in Hell not a span long swimming on the backs of devils centuries old'). The religion of Jesus, he said, was a happy one. 'It is music. It is love.'

He appeared in velvet or in a shooting jacket, and poked fun at the dark clothes of his colleagues whom he called 'sky pilots': an extraordinary use of metaphor in the empty skies of the mid-nineteenth century, but then he did not seem part of his age at all. At the height of the Temperance Movement he smoked and drank and gloried in both. Awarding prizes at his old theological college in Carmarthen, he chose instead to address the exam failures. 'I was here in this place many years ago and I never won a prize in my life,' he told them cheerfully. 'And I can speak English by the yard now.'

He encouraged his countrymen to acquire 'the language of beef steak and plum pudding', publishing a grammar in which he wished them 'good luck in your efforts to learn, speak and write in the language of the Englishman'. He would not have been part of the Welsh Establishment in our time. He was fresh air and life, and men treasured anecdotes about him. Accused at college of having been to the races, he told the authorities that this was so, but it had been in deference to the precept 'Prove all things, hold fast to that which is good'. He had found the races bad, he declared, and would not be going again.

Alas, they have forgotten him in the little chapel at Kilsby now, just as everywhere they have forgotten the great preachers. 'I don't reckon to go beyond fifteen minutes in a sermon,' said the present pastor, who has two other chapels in his ministry. 'This is the television generation. People don't read, so sitting and listening is difficult for them . . .'

But close your eyes for a moment and try to see the great preacher in this pulpit he occupied for ten years. He was not a good pastor, he said once, because he found he could not like all men equally. This was a man completely without humbug, who did not give a damn. He was capable of laughter.

III: The Chapel Closed at Christmas

Now here's a Christmas story. As electric stars flash over a hundred shopping malls and carols get cranked out in a thousand towns, something that has nothing to do with commerce is coming to an end in Northamptonshire. Today, after 136 years, the last service will be held in the Methodist chapel in the village of Maidford.

I was brought up among such places – indeed, have been on the run from them for most of my adult life – but when one goes I find myself very moved. I remember that line when Shirley MacLaine, I think it is, turns to Robert Mitchum and proposes that they run away together. At this the old eyelids jerk up like a window blind. 'Why, who's chasing us?' Where will the guilt come from in a world without chapels?

It was such a small chapel, hardly bigger than the lounge in a modern house. And no stained glass, no memorial plaques, none of the wistful little thrills of the Old Descent, just bare walls, a pulpit smaller than the desks of company chairmen, fading varnish on the pews. But of course it was small: non-conformity never had more than a handhold in these villages of gentry and farm labourers. Men whose ancestors had worshipped in the fields built chapels wherever a piece of ground could be found, always in brick, for the squire denied them the stone pits. But however small they were, these were the seedbeds of Radicalism. Where a chapel closes, a chapter of history closes with it.

'I grew up in a time when chapels didn't close,' said the minister, the Revd Ted Hawton, who himself retires next year. 'And now they are.' But what is bewildering is the speed with which it is happening, because non-conformity, at its high tide in the villages 100 years ago, does not share the slow stately decline of the established church; it is in a nosedive. Some chapels are converted into private houses, others drift from one use to another. The chapel in our village, for years a car showroom, is an art gallery now.

'I was married in that car showroom,' said the Organist gently. An ex-lorry driver, he has been a member of Maidford chapel since 1929 and has played the organ, a small pedal job, since he was fifteen. In those sixty-five years there have been only four weddings, two of them of his own daughters, but as for funerals . . . 'Oh, no end of funerals,' said the Organist.

The way he said this reminded me of the time I called at Farthingstone Baptist Chapel, also brick, also very small, and, finding a lady cleaning it, I asked her where they held their baptisms now. 'Baptisms?' she said. 'Oh, we shan't have to worry about baptisms ever again.'

Mind you, sometime earlier I had called at that same chapel and asked an older lady whether it might be possible to look round. 'No,' she had said, and I loved that: it was the voice of the old intolerant non-conformity which had no experience of dilettante strangers. So the deacons of Bancyfelin Methodist Chapel might have answered, who during the Great War bombarded the War Office with telegrams insisting that no soldiers from the village be allowed rum in the trenches. Killed, yes, drunk, never. They were hot on sexual matters, too. My father told me the story of a local girl who gave birth out of wedlock. Her name was called out from the Big Seat where the deacons sat, and she was obliged to walk up the long aisle out of the chapel and out of the religious life of her entire community. But that was a long time ago, and in another country.

Tolerance had come by my time, though I can remember an argument about Heaven with my Sunday school teacher, a jeweller. I was fifteen and a pain. Would Socrates go to Heaven? Was Socrates a Christian? No. Then he would not go to Heaven. But Socrates was a good man. Well, if he was a good man he wouldn't be far from Heaven. Like Abergwili? This was a village two miles away. The jeweller was a patient man. Quite possibly Socrates would be living in somewhere like Abergwili.

Sunday school stopped about two years ago in Maidford. The Organist's daughter tried to get this going in the church but that failed too, for parents no longer sent their children to Sunday school. The Organist's own life was so bound up with the chapel that evening services were cancelled when he went on to night shifts. But it wasn't numbers that did for them in the end, it was damp, one wall giving the sort of meter-reading you would expect to find today in a state room on the *Titanic*. Repairs could not be justified.

The Organist peered out at the little vegetable patch behind the chapel where he, and his father before him, had planted cabbages, this year's crop being one of the best ever. It was odd, he said, to see it end like this.

IV: Let Us Spray

I T I S A N odd moment in the life of a village when its chapel undergoes a building conversion. Oh, yes, there are jokes. The Baptists will continue to use its graveyard so, uniquely in a modern village, one man, his conversion completed, will be unable to escape knowing his neighbours. Their calling cards, in black marble, will lay siege to his house. But there is unease, too. For when a man sees a chapel go, he starts to worry about what will go next in the village. The school? The shop? The pub? The heap of sand at the chapel door is an unmistakable pointer to the end of things, and no man likes to encounter an index to his own life.

It is happening very quickly. Within a 10-mile radius, I know of an enormous place built by the Methodists, those Stalinists of non-conformity, which has become a nightclub; and another, a neat Baptist chapel, currently a car showroom, which now, with its garage owners pulling out of the village, will probably end up as a house. But how do you make a house out of a chapel?

'With difficulty,' said Andrew Bryant. Mr Bryant has bought a small

1813 Baptist chapel in a hamlet near my home, and hopes to move in within two years. It will be his second chapel conversion, divorce having deprived him of the first one. Mr Bryant is a solo guitarist, which made me think of the Elvis Presley hit 'Crying in the Chapel'. They were not that expensive, he told me, with prices ranging between £10,000 and £40,000. It was not their size that determined the price (he had heard of one in North Wales with planning permission for five flats on the market for £15,000), but matters such as parking and access to roads. Chapels, murmured Mr Bryant, got built in funny places.

'You can make a lot of mistakes,' he said, sitting in his vestry, surrounded by packing cases and memorials to the dead on the walls above him, some of them names I recognised. An exotic figure with his hair in the sort of pigtail favoured by Nelson's Navy, he chose at that moment to sing a sad little song about answerphones, accompanying himself on his guitar. 'Words by me, music by Bach,' said Mr Bryant.

Architecturally, chapels tend to be large rectangular halls, their beams usually an A-frame. The first thing a new owner wants is an upper floor, so what does he do? He chops through the centre of the A to make head room, at which point the walls start to move in. 'You see the cracks at the end of the first month,' said Mr Bryant. Then there are the various forms of rot. Conditions are perfect for this behind the half-panelling of chapels, especially with the building being heated up one day a week and the moisture left for the other six. 'I have it all here,' said Mr Bryant proudly. 'I have wet rot, dry rot, ordinary beetle and even an oversized beetle.' He pulled away some of the panelling and the yellow spores hung in fronds like Spanish Moss in the swamps of Louisiana. 'All this wood will have to be burnt out of doors. And when I spray, I shall not be able to live in that part for a year.'

As we talked, there were men outside digging a grave. Unless the chapel is very old, the graveyard does not get sold with it, especially when, as in this case, there is a waiting list of the living. Mr Bryant has thus done a deal whereby he builds them a new gate and they allow him a piece of earth as a parking space. He showed me where the land on the other side had been cut into to give parking spaces to a nearby terrace of council houses, thus revealing the foundations of the chapel, which, since then, have begun to crumble and will have to be underpinned.

He beamed as I walked away. I felt I had met a happy man.

1994, 1995

PART SIX

TALES
OF
THE PARANORMAL,
THE MACABRE
AND THE BIZARRE

Don't Mess with the Paranormal

THE LETTER WAS from a man describing himself as a research worker in the supernatural ('Every building has a tale to tell, every standing stone its secret. All that is needed to hold converse with them is to know the language of death . . .'). I showed it to my friend Geraint Morgan. 'Shouldn't touch that,' said Geraint. 'Let me tell you a story, they're not open yet.'

It had been a terrible winter evening, the rain like a cinema curtain on his windscreen as he drove to Stratford after an examiners' meeting in Oxford (Geraint is an academic). This was before the M40, on the old A34 where it goes serpentine after Woodstock. So there were lorries and mud, and he was finding it hard to see the road when he looked at his watch and saw it was 6.30. 'Time for a livener,' he said to himself.

Now it doesn't matter much where the village is. You will all have seen such places strung out along a trunk road, a shading of council estates, a few bungalows, one or two large houses around the heavily Gothicisised church, just somewhere on the way to somewhere else. As you drive through it occurs to you that you have never stopped here and never will. Yet Geraint knew where the pub was. With some people it is castles that register, with others churches, but with him it is pubs. He may only have driven through a village once or twice but give him its name and he will tell you the name of the pub. Even though, like this one, it was the most forgettable pub on earth. There were no carpets, just linoleum. No beer mats of any kind. One single strip light and a small electric fire beside which a young man sat reading a book. The landlady, a woman in her sixties, was knitting something long and grey behind the bar. The two were not talking.

Geraint had bought a pint when it occurred to him that the landlady had not said a word to him either, just pulled the beer and given him his change. A very large man, Geraint likes to talk to people in pubs. He sat down by the fire and nodded to the young man. 'Come far?'

'The Medway ports.'

He was, Geraint noticed, wearing slippers, and was polite enough, even though he did not look up from his book. 'Fair way then. You a sailor?'

'No, I'm a psychiatric male nurse.' He was a fat young man and very pale.

Geraint finished his drink and ordered another. He could hear a clock ticking very loudly out the back. 'I suppose you get a lot of people like us, passing trade,' he said to the landlady, jerking his head back to include the man. But as he did so he saw he wasn't there anymore, though the book lay face down on the chair.

'Oh no, he's a regular.'

'He just told me he comes from the Medway.'

'He does, but any time he can get off he comes up here.'

Geraint stared at her in case she might be joking, but there was no sign of that. She had one of these thin faces which get pointed at you as though the owner is forever asking a question.

'This is one of the most famous haunted inns in England. A young girl was starved to death here, not that anyone ever sees her. It's . . . everything else.'

Geraint nodded vaguely, convinced now he had fallen among lunatics. He walked over to the chair, read *Parameters of the Paranormal* on the book's spine and, turning over the pages, saw underlinings in green Biro. He put it down carefully as though it might spill. 'I don't suppose you've got such a thing as a pork pie?'

'We don't do food,' said the woman.

He took a packet of fags out. 'Smoke?'

'Oh no, I promised my husband.'

Geraint waved his hand in the air. 'Well, he's not here, is he?'

'Oh yes, he is.' The thin old face was run out a few inches more. 'His hand's on mine now. It's been like that ever since he died three months ago. He looks after me.'

Curiously, that conversation having hit the buffers, she then began to talk about the village's need for a bypass. There was still no sign of the male nurse, but she asked Geraint if he would like to see the haunted room before he went. 'Did you go?' I asked.

'Oh yes, and if the bar was bleak, you should have seen the upstairs. Not an ornament anywhere and no lampshades, just bare electric bulbs. We went down this corridor and she opened a door and we went into a room with a single bed – you could almost reach out and touch the damp. There were no clothes anywhere, but on a little table beside the bed there was this glass with a single set of dentures in it. I said it was a bit chill. "*Chill?*" she said and suddenly she was coming towards me. "Don't you understand I've got the central heating going full blast? And there's nothing . . . *nothing* we can do about it. Of course it's chill."'

'What happened then?' I asked.

'Nothing, that was the odd bit. We went downstairs and she made me a cup of coffee. People are as good as gold if you can keep them off the hereafter. That's why I'd throw the letter away. A port and brandy, don't you think?'

1993

The Thing in the Wood

THE TREES ARE so close together, 70-, 80-, 100-foot sycamores barrelling upwards, jostling and frantic for the sun, that even at noon there is no shadow, for what light there is in the wood comes through the green filter of their foliage. But at evening . . . when you enter the wood at evening, in a silence where a dead branch cracks underfoot like a whip, your eyes find it so hard to adjust to the gloom that, in the middle of England with the wind carrying the sound of traffic on the M1, you could be in a rain forest. But you are not in a rain forest: long ago man was in this place. *All around you are the remains of colossal fortifications, and, however often you come here, the scale of them always takes the breath away.*

'I was in the pub one night, and this young chap from the village, he's something to do with computers, asked if he could walk his girlfriend's dog there.' Since 1950 the wood has belonged to the family of Robert Tate of Farthingstone, near Daventry. 'I told him to go ahead. But when I met him a few days later he had a wild look about him. "That bloody wood of yours," he said. "If you were to pay me £5,000, I wouldn't go there again." He'd gone up there with the dog in a car he'd borrowed from a friend, parked this and taken the dog into the wood. Big dog it was and all.

'But no sooner were they inside than the thing started acting up, looking around it, hackles, and suddenly, whoosh, it was off, him chasing after it out of the wood and across the field. When he caught up with it, the dog had wriggled under the car and it was trembling. But it wasn't that. It had been so desperate to get inside, the dog had clawed at the doors and the bonnet. "That wood of yours, it cost me £200 in bodywork," he said.'

> . . . *If you enter the woods*
> *Of a summer evening late* . . .

The wood used to belong to the Russell family, who still farm nearby. In front of their house is something they got out of the wood and which old farmer Russell once described to me as a stone coffin; they have filled this with earth and flowers grow in it. They had to move it on rollers, he told me, for this is solid stone, the length of a man, which has been hollowed out. The Romans buried their dead in such things, and later the men of the early Middle Ages their grandees. But this is no stone coffin. It has the dimensions and the craft all right, but one side of it is in the shape of a bow. If something was buried in that, it would not have been shaped like a man.

Eric James, now seventy, has lived all his life in a farmhouse in the field next to the wood; it, and whatever is inside it, is a matter of 30 yards away. 'We had an Army training school up here during the War, and it was so tough the troops dreaded it, some of them got killed here. And I remember this Major Harrison, he'd heard stories about the wood, and he was so fascinated by them he was going to let a mine off in the middle of it. Not a bomb, a *mine*. He said he was going to find out once and for all what was there. Of course it was the War, you could do such things, but at the last minute even he drew back. There are so many stories.'

In 1712 the Revd John Morton, compiling his *Natural History of Northamptonshire*, met workmen who had dug for stone there to build the house in which Mr James now lives. The centre of their activity was the great mound in the middle of the wood, on the slopes of which you can still see cut stone covered with green lichen. 'Those Workmen,' wrote the Revd Morton crossly, 'do not agree in the Account of what was met with there.' This, you will note, is not a story handed on and embellished; it is a recorded eyewitness account. Morton set down those things on which the men were agreed, that as they had dug down into the mound, they found themselves in a stone room, the walls of which were covered with a coat of lime. They put a ladder in the floor so they could carry the stones up, but as one of them was doing this, the ladder suddenly began to sink, until eight or nine steps of it had disappeared and he himself was up to his waist. For below the first room was another, 'out of which arose a smell like that of putrid carcasses . . .' Even today there is something a bit strange about this mound, for its summit is a saucer-like depression about 5 feet deep, as though something had indeed collapsed there, then been filled with earth, just as Morton said.

So where are we? On a map of Northamptonshire find the village of Farthingstone, then follow the back road to Weedon. If you can imagine the map dissolving into the landscape, the way maps do in films, you will find yourself climbing a steep hill, with fields of wheat about you. Some 300 yards past the first crossroads you will be on a plateau with the wood on your right, but to go further you will need the permission of Mr Robert Tate, a man who, to his bewilderment, found he had inherited a very old mystery.

'My father bought it as part of a 90-acre farm. This was derelict land then, all slit trenches and undergrowth after the War, so bad you couldn't even walk across it. And, of course, in the middle of it were these 11 acres, eight acres of wood and three of this field with all the ridges round it.' Mr Tate opened a large envelope marked English Heritage. Every year the letters come, reminding him what he can and can't do with these 11 acres. 'Mustn't excavate, mustn't let anyone onto them with a metal detector. This chap asked, "Mind if me and the boy ran a detector over that wood?" "Not if you don't mind going down for ten years." "Bloody hell," he said. All I can do is plough that three-acre field, they let me do that, but even there I mustn't plough more than seven inches deep.'

The track runs down through a linseed field to where, seven inches down, Mr Tate has planted winter wheat. You can see a very long way from up here, the lorries on Watling Street, the sunlight reflected in the windows of cars using the M1 beyond, as England, her waist drawn in, passed below you on roads and railways and canals, all of them not three miles from each other. So whoever built that Thing in the Wood knew exactly what he was doing: it dominates the landscape which streams away from it. Yet even now you can stand here and not see a single human habitation. The emptiness of Northamptonshire is its most extraordinary feature.

What you can see is the first fortification, banks of earth 20 feet high enclosing Mr Tate's wheat in a rectangle with rounded corners, 100 yards by 150. This is the first mystery. There is a geometric precision to it that you don't get in the Middle Ages or in the Iron Age. But the Roman legions built their camps in rectangles like this.

At this point you still have no idea what awaits you at the far end of the field, where the wood begins. It looks like a hedge, but when you get to it you find yourself peering down, down, into green depths, and for the first time you realise the scale of this place. Now the 40-foot ramparts begin. You are entering a fortification crouched inside the wood which, with the rectangle, covers an area not far short of Windsor Castle.

A causeway crosses the ditch, bisecting the first rampart, and then the labyrinth begins, with even higher ramparts writhing in and out of each other, so that at the south-east there are four lines of them, one behind the other. In the green twilight you see these banks of earth, and in the very centre the huge man-made hill. Had anyone attacked this place they would have been led on deeper and deeper into the ditches, at every turn of which there would have been men about them. For it is not a matter of concentric rings: these fortifications lure you inside and there is no way out. But who built them and when?

'There are many entrenchments, the whole compass whereof contains about 11 acres of ground,' wrote Morton. 'And in the highest part thereof there stood a Castle, or however a Structure of Strength, or of Note, upon that entrenched Hill, this appearing plainly by the stones that have been digged up there . . .' But what was it? Morton didn't know. 'It does not appear to have been of Roman Erection,' he began carefully enough. 'And had it been built or demolished since the Norman Conquest, we should in all likelihood have heard of it, either from History or Tradition, which we never have . . .' It had to be Saxon, he ventured, probably demolished by the Danes, when the valley beneath was a war zone and Watling Street an international border. If pushed, he went on recklessly, he would give it the date 913.

'It is a medieval motte and bailey castle, probably of the late eleventh to twelfth century,' said Glenn Foard, the Northants County Archaeologist. 'But it is a massive castle, and what is unusual is that it is in such an isolated place. There is no documentary evidence of any kind for it, so we don't know the names of who built or even owned it. What we do know is that it was in use for a considerable length of time, for it had stone buildings. But there has been no modern excavation of any kind.'

Others are more circumspect. 'This large earthwork represents a medieval castle,' wrote Pevsner, the authority on architecture, confidently enough, but then he faltered, '. . . of a comparatively unusual type.' The Royal Commission on Ancient Monuments hedged its bets even more remarkably. It was a motte and bailey, it began. 'However it is probable that part of its outer ramparts are of Iron Age origin.' In other words, the Thing in the Wood swings wildly across 1000 years.

Iron Age Britons. The fortifications would not have been beyond them. Archaeologists using primitive tools, deer antler picks to break the soil, shoulder blades of oxen to shovel it out, have shown that one man could build 12 cubic feet of bank and ditch in a day, so 150 men could fortify an eight-acre enclosure with a single bank and ditch in four months. But that is just a single bank. The multiple ramparts, and the complex fortification, might be the defenders' answer to the new weapon that came in two centuries before Christ, the sling, which could send a rounded stone half the size of a billiard ball some 200 yards. Yet why would they have abandoned this place?

No real mystery here. Look down and you see Watling Street, the old Roman road. From here one day 2000 years ago a man would have seen coming up the valley floor something which just wasn't possible, 6000 men *in formation and in silence*, a Roman legion on the move. Imagine the terror of that to men for whom armies would have been an untidy mob. I read somewhere a POW's account of the day American tanks were seen, of how the German sentry stared, let his rifle fall to the ground, then strolled quietly away. Something like that might have happened here, in a hill fort which until then had been impregnable. But so impregnable it might have been used again.

The flat rectangle looks like a Roman vallum. The central motte is probably medieval, for the Thing in the Wood, though there would not have been a wood then, was a ready-made fortress. They had everything up there, even a spring, for in the quiet you can hear the sound of water. In troubled times, once you had got over your fear of ghosts, all you had to do was move in and let it out at the seams.

'They say the road in front of our farm was very important once,' said Mrs Russell. It is a small country lane, with barely enough room for two cars to pass, but once men called it the Great Street or the Old Salt Way, and you can see the packhorses moving slowly. And now, who comes now? 'I think you are the only one this year,' said Eric James. 'Last year an American came, said he'd come all the way from Denver, Colorado.'

So there is no litter, apart from the odd torn fertiliser sack, and a single, empty tin of talcum powder. It is a place where, on the rare occasion it calls, mankind pauses to tear up a few old sacks, powder its bottom thoughtfully, then move on. But once . . . who knows, who will ever know?

1999

Mr Batten Buys a Castle

I

SOME BOUGHT CARS, others treated themselves to the holidays they had only dreamt about until then: when the building societies became banks, most people regarded their windfall profit as so much fairy gold. But one man, an old-age pensioner in Northamptonshire, bought a local castle.

And not any castle. He will never move in – there is nothing to move into – for long before men built in stone, his castle stood, a thing of wood and mud, of which only the mud remains. 'Got your wellingtons?' asked Derek Batten, who has bought himself a medieval ringwork.

'Look at the *size* of it,' said Mr Batten, with awe. The great mound towered above us, 40 feet from moat to rampart. 'It's vast and it's *mine*,' said the new owner of Alderton Castle, and it could have been that scene in Western films where the cattle baron surveys his domain.

Earlier he had told me why he had bought it. There was the need to safeguard the site, said Mr Batten, who is a county councillor. Then there was public access to weigh against the possibility of an archaeological dig. He managed to make it sound as though there was a public obligation on every man to buy a castle.

'Come off it,' I said. 'You bought it because you're a romantic.'

'I bought it because I'm a romantic,' said Derek Batten.

His study is dominated by a large painting of Custer's Last Stand (which would have been more successful had he, too, had a castle), next to which, in line, hang sepia photos of the heroes of the Old West, the Indians and the gunfighters. Mr Batten, a retired surveyor, is the only Englishman to have worked on the excavation of the battle site of Little Big Horn. He is also probably the only living Englishman to have bought a mound.

He was driving past it last summer when he saw the sign. Mr Batten in his time had seen many estate agents' signs, but never one like this: 'For Sale, Moat and Castle'. What made it even more bizarre was that until then he had not even known there was a castle there, two miles from his home. It must be 700 years since its last lord, wistful for warmth, walked down from the mound and into a manor house. The road runs past but there is a bend in it at this point, so no one looks up. If they chance it and do, they will think it some intractable agricultural feature behind the trees.

Who built it, nobody knows: probably some landless Norman thug who had ridden up Watling Street and, using forced labour, was staking his claim here. The sheer size of his castle, 1.72 acres of it, showed he meant business. And he must have prospered, for the village and the church at its foot are still here, a row of new houses so close a garden has been quietly extended on to its slopes. But the castle, like most castles, is unknown to history.

'Because of its great age [we] have so far been unable to discover if it was the site of any battles,' sighed the estate agent, in what is a classic perspective even by the standards of his curious profession. 'It may be possible to recreate the medieval wooden buildings . . .' Oh yeah, tell that to English Heritage. 'There will be provision for the sellers to share in any future finds of treasure . . .' Then the guide price, arrived at God knows how: £10,000 to £20,000.

Part of a royal hunting estate, the old castle was owned by dukes, then by barons, until a local farmer bought a parcel of land and found this contained something even he dared not plough up. The castle had become a Scheduled Ancient Monument. Then Mr Batten, his Halifax money burning a hole in his pocket, came up the road. Oh rash Mr Batten . . . Once he would have held this by the sword (or, in his case, the genuine Seventh Cavalry Carbine which he owns), but ever since he bought the castle a month ago, bureaucrats have been calling on Mr Batten on his mound.

English Heritage has called and the Heritage officers of both county and district councils. The Tree Preservation man has come to check on the sycamores, the Wildlife Trust man to check on the badgers. Soon the bat man will come and various ecological officers, for when you acquire a mound in England, you acquire a social round. 'I insured it this week,' said Mr Batten. 'I went into a brokers' and they blinked a bit, but I now have £1 million third-party cover on my castle. My first premium was £132.50.'

As we tramped round the mound, I in suedes, Mr Batten in wellingtons, he told me he planned to leave his castle to the nation. He talked about the unevenness of the ground in which you could see foundations from a time when this was the centre of a little world. He talked about the views that would return when the trees were felled. But mostly he talked about its size. 'I mean, just *look* at it.'

I looked, and slipped and cursed and listened. In the church below us the oldest thing by far is the oak effigy of an unknown medieval knight, the last lord of the castle. Out of a long exile his improbable successor has returned.

II

HE TOOK A friend up one evening and began to talk about how one day guided parties of schoolchildren might come, and how open-air performances of *A Midsummer Night's Dream* could be held under the sycamores. When he paused, something he does not often do, the man looked at him. 'Derek, it's just a great big toy.'

It is an expensive one. He cleared the waist-high scrub, and the skip hire alone cost him £100. He installed wooden steps, for he had no wish to seal his castle off, and they cost £1,000. So far the tree clearance, agreed with the council, has cost him £2,100. And that was the first row. He addressed a village meeting and even published a management plan, but no one reads a management plan. The village assumed he was going to fell all the trees and a petition was got up against him.

'But it had never been my intention and I had said so. I only took down twelve trees out of 150, and even then I planted 400 little trees around the perimeter of the moat. That cost £600. I laid out piles of wood chips under a sign, "People of Alderton, help yourselves." And they did, but unfortunately not enough of them, for the bloody peacocks landed in the wood chips and cut their feet.' Nobody is sure who owns the peacocks. There are three of them, they roam the village, and, not only did they cut their feet, they managed to break their legs on the logs, which brought the television programme *Pet Rescue* to Alderton.

Then there was the row with the people who had extended their gardens up the castle mound during the years of neglect. Not content with that, they have now laid a rope interwoven with electric wire right up to the ramparts, thus staking a claim to future expansion. They argue that this was under something called Adverse Possession, since nobody had questioned their right to do so in the past. Mr Batten, who thought that English Heritage would sort this out for him, found they would not.

'If they built anything like a fence up there, we'd be on them like a ton of bricks,' said Dr Glyn Coppach of English Heritage. 'But gardening does not affect the archaeology. What it is, is bloody annoying in that it affects the appearance of the site, but unfortunately that's his problem, not ours. Would I buy a castle? NEVER. But it will be a cracking dilemma for the lawyers.'

Which is where the matter now rests, Mr Batten gloomily totting up his costs to date. He has had signs put up, 'Please Take Care When Walking Around this Mount.'

He has had pamphlets printed, listing the mysteries of Alderton ('Why is it there? How long has it been there? Why is it so big?'). He has addressed meetings of headmasters, hoping they would bring their pupils to see the castle, but so far no one has taken up his free offer.

'Bless him, he's tried so hard,' said Margaret Hall-Townley of Alderton. 'He's put the steps in so we don't slide down the mound. It's a wonderful place, like a little island in the midst of all this farmland. You get sightings of some very unusual birds up there, the children love it, they sit under the trees. And now the whole village is very excited.'

For the television archaeological programme *Time Team* is coming. Pippa Gilbert, a programme researcher and a veteran of such digs as Lindisfarne, where they hoped to find evidence of early Christianity but instead found a brewery, was on her third visit to Alderton, in the course of which she has met many of its inhabitants. 'You have to remember what it'll mean for them when three camera crews, a production team, a range of experts and the caterers descend on them. It is going to be a major inconvenience. But everyone I've met is looking forward to it.'

'Even the besieging gardeners?'

'Even the gardeners,' said Miss Gilbert carefully.

One man awaits their coming as the inhabitants of Fort Bridger, with half the Sioux nation howling outside, awaited the bugles in the afternoon. 'I haven't had the fun I expected with my castle,' said Derek Batten. 'I just hope this changes everything.'

1999

The House from Hansel and Gretel

I<small>T WAS QUITE</small> possibly the best thing the man at the Forestry Commission had heard that day. 'You found this little house in the woods? And it was a log cabin with French windows, and it had graves around it? I see. You didn't by any chance meet an old lady who offered you gingerbread?'

We shouldn't have been in the woods. The 'Footpath' sign at the gate was at such an angle we thought someone had turned it, a much-loved country pastime, and we did not notice the gap in the undergrowth to which it pointed at the edge of the field. All we saw was the wood in front of us, its gate tied with twine. All gates are around here, except those on land owned by men who spend the week in the City. So we went on.

On one side of the path the wood was a real Forestry Commission place, all Germanic gloom, brown pine needles, shadow and nothing living at all. It had to be one of theirs, or some pop star's tax shelter. It is accountancy, not teddy bears, that you meet in the woods today. But on the other side the wood was different. It had green undergrowth and trees that accountants do not plant – copper birch, willow, poplar – and we got nervous. This place had clearly meant something to someone and might do so again.

And then we came on something that had no business in a wood. The pond was ornamental, for you could see where it had been dug, but successive droughts had done for it, and we could see where rabbits had tunnelled into the sides. Just past this, in what must once have been a clearing, was the house.

It was an immaculate little log cabin, the logs cut and stacked with care. Two French windows formed the door, so its origins appeared to be partly *Good Housekeeping*, partly Arthur Rackham's illustrations for fairytales. A witch might have lived there, who would have used an Elizabeth David recipe to cook her gingerbread, but it was clear no one had lived there for some time.

No path led to it; the nettles were chest high. As I hacked my way through, I saw strange bits of ornamental stone in the undergrowth, staddlestones and something that might have been a bird bath. Through the French windows I saw folding canvas chairs of the sort film directors use, and on one was an open magazine from the top shelf of some newsagent. This, at least, was familiar: you cannot go into an English wood these days without finding porn in a hollow tree or showing out of a badger's set. 'Can't be much fun being a badger,' said my doctor. 'There you are leading a quiet family life, and the next minute someone's stuffed a six-month run of *Fiesta* up your back passage.'

Whoever had left it must have been a trespasser like us, for when the door opened as I tried the handle, I came into a panelled pine room with a row of books – H.E. Bates, Osbert Sitwell, a collection of fairytales. There was also a camping-gas burner and something which would only have meant one thing to our ancestors had they found it in a house in the woods, and even now was very strange. It was a tiny male doll – but this was 1996 and it was an Action Man toy. One last thing I saw – some mounds in a glade next to the house. Whoever had used the place had also dug some small graves near his front door.

At the pub they were suspicious when I asked my very careful questions. Had I been after the rabbits? No. What was I doing in the wood then? I had lost my way. Ah. No, nobody knew who owned it. I did not mention the house.

But since then I have learned its story. The wood was owned by an old lady, comfortably off and unmarried, who bought it because she wanted to own one. 'Nice to have a wood of your own,' said her nephew. And here she had a summerhouse built where she could come with friends, sometimes on her own, to drink tea and read or just sit. Under the trees she buried her pet dogs. They had played there as children, said her nephew. But after his aunt's death, ten years ago, they had rarely been, for it was felt something had come to an end there. Yes, she might well have offered her guests gingerbread. So now I have a phone call to make.

It is to the Forestry Commission, and it will give me great pleasure.

1996

The Witch's House

W E C A M E D O W N from the ridge to get out of the wind. That had
been like a filleting knife up there, so even the old ruin below us
had looked cosy in the natural amphitheatre of the park. Then I saw something glint in the later afternoon sun.

A metal barrier had been put up all round the house, and the undergrowth stripped away. Symbols screamed that this was now a hard-hat
area, and old stones and tiny Tudor bricks were stacked in neat piles.
After an interval of 300 years the builders were in at the Witch's House.

My daughter called it that when she was small, for she knew exactly
where she was. She was in the world of her *Rupert* books. No road led to
the house; it just stood, or rather lent, at a terrifying angle in the grass,
with its strange little tower and barley-sugar chimneys. Stories were told
that on New Year's Eve a green huntsman rode out of it, blowing his horn,
and death followed for anyone who saw him. 'Spent a night there when I
was a boy, hoping to see the bugger,' said an old countryman. 'There was
no sign of him but I almost passed out from cold, so that bit might be
right.'

Nearby was the Wood of Mystery, at the entrance to which was a
solitary stone arch under which would have driven a carriage and pair. But
this led nowhere, the drive having disappeared under the mud and dead
trees. Two centuries ago Capability Brown bustled through the park,
conjuring up lakes and groves, but he was long gone, and the family that
had commissioned him had also gone, the last of them before World War
II. Reeds had run wild in the lakes, great trees no longer knew their
place.

Every detail was mysterious. The Welsh pamphleteer John Penry, later
hanged, took refuge in the house after his Martin Marprelate letters had
attacked the bishops in Elizabeth I's time. He was seen walking here in a

sky-blue cloak, an odd disguise for anyone on the run. In Victorian times the Elephant Man also sought refuge, his train being met by a shuttered carriage. Solitary and unmobbed, his time in the park must have been as close to normal life as the poor devil ever got.

But the Witch's House I never could figure out. It was behind the hills above the big house and, according to Pevsner, was already in ruins around 1710. They called it The Dower House, so either the family's supply of dowagers dried up, or it had been built for a purpose that no longer applied. And that is the clue.

It was early Tudor but built of two different materials and in two different styles. It had the appearance of a large H, an ironstone hall from which a passageway led to a brick structure with a tower. This is the earliest known use of brick in Northamptonshire, but for what? The current archaeological dig, part of a £260,000 Lottery Fund grant made by English Heritage, has begun to yield some answers.

The brick part was built first and for a specific purpose. The Witch's House was a Tudor hunting lodge. The tower was for ladies to watch the deer hunt, or even, as was the aristocratic custom delighted in by the first Elizabeth, to take pot shots with crossbows as the animals were driven past.

So why was it abandoned? Possibly because there were no more deer to hunt. An odd fact that has not surfaced in the fox-hunting controversy is that fox-hunting only dates from the late seventeenth century, when there were no deer left in the parks of England, the scavenging unpaid soldiers of the Civil War having eaten the lot. And this estate was on the front-line between the armies.

So there was no longer any need for this place, which entered folklore and the long decay that is now being arrested. It will be restored as a ruin, the latest style in historical conservation. But its mystery dies.

1998

Lord Cobham's Terrible Joke

T HIS STARTS IN sunlight, as stories do when, as the Fat Boy said, 'I wants to make your flesh creep.' It starts with a recent news item in the *Daily Telegraph*, for after two and a half centuries the Chinese House has been brought back to Stowe by the National Trust as part of its restoration of the Park. A photograph shows a small red building among trees. But then a name appears. The House, says Tim Knox of the National Trust, was probably designed by Lord Cobham – the old soldier and friend of the poet Pope – who built an Arcadia at Stowe, commissioning Vanbrugh, Kent, Adam and Capability Brown to lay out the Park and its follies.

It was just that soon after Cobham's death in 1749, the Chinese House disappeared, but other things went with it, very peculiar things, this time from the shadows of Arcadia. Not the classical temples, the obelisks, the ornamental towers that great architects and landscapers built for him: these survive to this day, giving 221 acres in Buckinghamshire the skyline of Disneyworld. It was the things which they had not had a hand in that went, the buildings hidden in the trees. 'Lord Cobham did have his slightly jokey side,' says Tim Knox.

A tiny temple, the roof of which consisted of tortoise shells, so God alone knows how many of the creatures died for my Lord's whimsy. A Witch's House, a nightmare of asymmetry in a thicket, with frescoes showing witches at an orgy. The Temple of Venus, also among the trees, which had a lady sporting with satyrs, watched by her aged husband. All these were got rid of after Cobham's death.

He had a lean, frightening face, this man who had made his money out of the sacked towns of Marlborough's wars, also from marrying a brewery. Not an eighteenth-century face at all, but that of a modern man, the blue jowls out of place in a periwig. And not a man you

would ever like to meet.' You know about Cobham and the poachers?'
I said.

'I thought that was folklore,' said Tim Knox.

'Oh, no.'

It should be folklore. Two men from the nearby village of Silverstone
were caught poaching in the deer park at Stowe, and their wives hurried to
the Great House where the aged Cobham, granting them an audience, was
charm itself. He assured them their men folk would return the following
week and even named a day. And sure enough on that day they did come
back, a carter alighting with a special message from Lord Cobham to
remind them he had kept his word to the letter, and to ask the wives what
they wanted done with the two coffins he had in his cart.

The story has the polish of folklore . . . except that a witness comes in
the solid shape of the Revd J.E. Linnell, 'a fearer of God and of no one
else', who in old age, just before the Great War, wrote his memoirs, later
published as *Old Oak*. Linnell's father, born in 1795, was the Vicar of
Silverstone and buried one of the two widows.

Her name was Mary Adams, and she had lived on and on, dying at the
age of 102 – except that the old carpenter put on her coffin that she was
1002, telling the startled vicar that one and two noughts made one hundred, to which he had then added a two. A ludicrous detail like that prises
the account away from folklore.

J.E. Linnell's sister also remembered Mary Adams, who had never
recovered from the shock of that morning in 1748. A widow for eighty
years, she wore all her life the white apron she had worn then, darning it
until not an original thread was left. This went to the grave with her.
According to Linnell, Cobham, the great aesthete, had lifesize figures cast
in red from the two bodies, one with a deer on his shoulders. These he
added to the statues already in Arcadia, the piping fawn, Hercules, and the
wounded gladiator, things to while away an afternoon when his smart
London friends came visiting.

What became of the two statues is not known, for they do not figure in
any of the sale catalogues printed as the estate was dispersed. They may
have been sold as just another job lot of mythology by an auctioneer who

did not know their origin. They may even have gone as soon as Cobham's nephew inherited, along with the strange little buildings in the trees, for there were certain things a man walking in Stowe Park did not wish to encounter by day or night. Lord Cobham did have his slightly jokey side.

1998

Voices in the Church

THIS HAPPENED a few days ago, yet I feel obliged at the outset to give you the sort of guarantee that Gulliver gave his reader: 'I could perhaps have astonished thee with wild improbable tales but I have chosen rather to relate plain matter of fact in the simplest manner and style; because my principal design was to inform and not to amuse thee.' There is another guarantee: it happened to me.

It started with the Chinese takeaway van. Most evenings this comes to the town of Towcester, and it fascinates me that from the interior of something smaller than a Ford Transit a man and his wife serve banquets. But on the night I drove to Towcester with my daughter, aged seven, there was no sign of it. It was 6.30 p.m. but, because everyone we asked assured us the van would be there by 7–7.30 p.m. at the latest, we started ambling round the town. Estranged because I refused to buy her an ice cream, we wandered separately down the lane to St Lawrence's Church, the name of that saint burnt alive in Rome over a gridiron, the coals from which the monks of Bury St Edmunds were still proudly displaying 1000 years later.

Now a church at seven on a summer's evening is something out of one of M.R. James's ghost stories. It is cool then, the shadows have come, there is the whiff of polish, and, if there is no one else there, the place is still as a rock pool. My daughter only agreed to come in when I agreed to buy noodles, not rice.

I was looking at some very old Bibles in a glass case and she was reading a poster illustrating Joseph's considerable wardrobe as an Egyptian civil servant when I heard the chanting. I turned to her and saw she, too, was looking around. It was men's voices, without musical backing, far away and faint, but not so faint that I could not make out that the words were in Latin and, I realised to my growing alarm, they were coming from somewhere deep underground. But before I go on, there is something you should know about me and this church.

Roughly five years ago I wrote about something its congregation would have preferred to keep secret. In the nave there is the tomb of an Archdeacon Sponne, one of those chaps who did well out of sheep during the Wars of the Roses and so could afford to have himself buried in what would have been a state-of-the-art tomb, a two-tiered High Gothic job, sculpted corpse on top and, underneath that, as the corpse would have looked after a year's decay.

Time passed, and in the 1980s the vicar of Towcester had a friend, also in holy orders and recently bereaved; to take his friend's mind off his loss he suggested that he paint Sponne. This was a staggering, if innocent, act of vandalism, for the friend painted him in Dulux and in Manchester United FC colours of red and white. What made it worse was that, at some point in the nineteenth century, the original wooden head had been removed (it was being kept in a hat box), and replaced with a huge Victorian stone head completely out of proportion with the medieval effigy. This head the friend painted the colour of tinned ham and on each large white eyeball placed a black blob so that, as I am afraid I wrote, a staring soccer loon seemed to be awaiting the Last Trump when he could leap up and nut his Creator.

There was, of course, a wonderfully muted Church of England row, with meetings of forgotten courts, and a restorer had to be called in for a five-figure sum to remove the paint. But the ham face and the mad eyes were for some reason left untouched, although the medieval head, now out of its hat box, was also put on show. I had even more fun with the two heads of Archdeacon Sponne.

The result was that I had been wary about entering the church, and also ever so slightly uneasy, half expecting . . . well, I'm not sure what, except that having read M.R. James in my youth I expect anything. And now, through the shadows, a chant which would have been familiar to Sponne was coming out of the ground near his tomb.

It is true, you know, what they say about fear. The little hairs really do stir at the back of your neck. But the chant was so beautiful I felt I had to go nearer. 'Don't,' said my daughter but, being too frightened to stay where she was, she slipped her hand into mine, a thing she only does now when we cross roads. We went forwards slowly, the chant increasing all the time but still faint. And then, to the side of the altar, we noticed a low stone arch beyond which were rounded steps leading downwards. We went through the arch on tiptoe and, there below us, we saw the singers and the sheets they were holding in the crypt.

'For a moment I thought I was going to see Jesus,' said my daughter, but she said that a long time later. That was after we had stopped blaming each other for the Chinese van, which in the end never came.

1990

PART SEVEN

THE VILLAGE AT PLAY

The Painting of the Hunt

THIS CONCERNS a moment. It is framed and hangs on the wall of a farmhouse kitchen where I see it every time I go for milk. The moment is a coloured cartoon, which, on 1 March 1933, formed the centre pages of the *Tatler*. The Reichstag had been burned down two days earlier, but Lord 'Bear' Hillingdon MFH sits his horse on the village green, his hounds about him, and the Grafton Hunt is meeting in the village of Blakesley. The old order stands.

'Hillingdon was a very tall thin man,' said the farmer. 'I think he lived for hunting. He financed the whole hunt, but not long after he lost all his money. Just after the war I saw him for the last time, when he turned up on a horse he'd borrowed locally, a rough old thing. I felt very sad.'

The farmer still remembers the first time he rode with the hunt. Two years had passed since the picture, and he was nine when the Grafton crossed his father's land and in short trousers and wellingtons he jumped on a pony to follow them. He remembers that day across fifty years because a lord spoke to him. Hillingdon said, 'Hello.'

But the farmer doesn't see the picture the way I do and you might, all those redundant captains with nicknames that were never explained to him: Captain 'Tiddly' Lucas, Captain 'Bush' Du Buisson. All he knows is that he was seven and, for a moment, in silk hats and red coats, the gods were on Mount Olympus. It is a very small mound – a child of three could climb it. But Lord 'Bear' is on its crest among the elms, and Lady 'Bear' with Mrs 'Bush' Du Buisson, who was an Honourable, and Mr 'Bovril' Pennington who rode in the Grand National. Below these the social order falls away, until in the foreground there is Mr George Beale, who merely owned a chain of grocery shops. Beale apart, the farmer does not know what any of the thirty did for a living. They were the gentry who owned fields and manor houses and mysterious things called shares, which ruined them. But the farmer, who now hunts with the Grafton himself, does know one thing: had he been there that day, he would not have been on the mound.

Nobody would have said anything to him, but then they would not have needed to in a time when there was a hunt ball and a quite separate hunt farmers' ball. But of the five joint masters of the Grafton, three are farmers now. For the old estates have been broken up, the farmers are landowners and the wind has blown the gods and the elms from the village mound, blowing away Captain 'Tiddly' Lucas, who drank a bottle of port a day and whose red nose is so delicately picked out by the cartoonist. The old TV commentator Dorian Williams's father has also gone, who once hired the Towcester brass band to play to his horses so they should know what lay ahead of them at the White City. And Miss Joan Broke, the only lady to ride astride that day. 'Oh, the talk, the muttering.' A rather intense revolutionary, Miss Broke is also wearing specs. The last from that picture, Captain 'Bush', who had one leg and was strapped to his saddle, died only a year ago, in his nineties. The village eccentric is also gone; he would turn up to every meet in full kit and then, as soon as the hunt moved off, ride quietly home, touching his cap to passers by, 'Goodnight', though it was noon.

Now the horses, which were once walked to every meet, arrive in pantechnicons like pampered invalids, and the long walks home in the mud and the sunset are relegated to Surtees and folklore. Today the jumps are choreographed as precisely as a ballet. 'Not then,' said the farmer. 'Then they jumped everywhere and rode everywhere, for the men in that picture, they owned everything.'

They stare into the middle distance, moustachioed, straight-backed, riding crops in their white-gloved hands, the gentlemen of England, doing just as their fathers had done, and their fathers before them. They would have thought things would always be like this. But the greatest architect of social change old England would ever know was waiting his hour. Adolf Hitler had been Chancellor of Germany for two months.

So the cartoonist Tout was the last herald of a doomed cast. I smile every time I see his picture. The farmer does not smile.

The Village Outing

NOBODY KNOWS for certain when this was. John Butler – that's John, at the extreme right of the back row in the one photograph, the thin-faced chap in the FBI trilby he had borrowed from his brother Fred for the day – thinks he was twenty then, which would mean it was around 1929. So Hitler was still a street agitator, Churchill a man with a great future behind him, the day the village choir on its first seaside outing went to Southsea.

The Outing. The word is fading, having been hijacked by militant homosexuals. Once it was the only form of holiday travel for most people in this country, the day out in the charabanc for the Sunday school or the works or the choir. See them there, like astronauts, not daring to venture far from the little bus with its fussy curtains, for this was their one link with home. And they remembered only too clearly that old Frank Loydell, the blacksmith, had missed the train home on the previous year's outing to the Wembley Exhibition; Mr Loydell, who stammered, did not turn up in the village until the next day. Look at those faces. Some of them were about to see the sea for the first time, for the village they came from is almost exactly in the middle of England, the bus the first owned by the local company. Now look at the holiday offers on the pages around you, and at the photograph again: in front of you is the travel business in its beginnings.

It does not matter where the village was, except it was 100 miles north of Southsea and it took the bus six hours to get there. 'We met at five in the morning, chattering like swallows, anxious to be off,' said John Butler. Nor does it matter who they were, the carpenter, the postmistress, the off-licence man. They could have been your grandparents or mine, except that a space on the war memorial waited for one of them.

But you must meet Frank, the man at the left of the back row, with the moustache like the old silent-film comedian Ben Turpin. He was the village plumber and, given his habit of taking away a souvenir from each job, its kleptomaniac. Frank went along as the bell-ringer, but the vicar did not come, 'not being a sociable man'.

Still, old Mr Constable, the builder, was at the bus stop, carrying a bag. The young choristers had been promised five shillings pocket money each, but Mr Constable, a man with a large beard, just nodded to them. 'Morning,' he said, as though it were the most natural thing in the world to be up at five, and walked on. Then he relented, grinned and began doling out the cash.

What follows is seen through John Butler's eyes. He is eighty-six now, a retired gardener ('You're looking at history, boy'), but the outing is as vivid as yesterday, with people like Frank and one young girl in a cloche hat whose father had a wooden leg ('he used to fight a chap with one eye outside the pub, when they could find each other').

They were all so excited they did not notice how long the journey took, but old Mr Webb the gardener did (who said in a loud voice as soon as the bus stopped, 'Can anyone tell me where the urinal is, please?'). They had talked about nothing but the outing for weeks, and as the clock ticked away even the cleaning of the church's oil lamps (a number seared into John Butler's brain) seemed no chore.

And what did they do in Southsea? 'Nothing much. Billy Kingston, the driver, had given us such a lecture about getting lost, we daren't go far.' Nobody swam, for nobody in the village owned a costume – or could swim. Nobody paddled either. 'Water were too deep, at least we thought it was. We just sat on the beach and picked up shells. To be honest, we must have looked lost. God knows what Southsea people made of these yokels who had fallen out of a bus and were sitting there, staring at the mighty sea.'

After a while they began to walk up and down the front, pondering on the awesome responsibilities of being on holiday. Some checked that they could remember the streets that led back to the bus, and when they met they greeted each other loudly. Nobody bought a meal – that was beyond their means – but those who had been too excited to eat their egg sandwiches on the way now began to eat them. And they were bored.

The sun shone but nobody took off his cap, and there was much synchronisation of fob watches, for the beach had begun to lose its novelty. 'Weren't much of a beach anyhow. Sea just flopped up right on the front. And the more we looked at it, the more we worried about missing the bus.' Somewhere there were strangers running in and out of the water and being noisy. But by mid-afternoon those on the outing had begun to gather in a larger and larger group, and the only one missing was Frank the plumber, a man who to this day fascinates John Butler. 'I never did find out what happened to him; he'd ferret anything out, he would. He had the whole world in his sights.'

The journey back, unlike the journey out, took forever, with England all hills and bends, the young cursing the rock they had eaten and the old trying to sleep. Nobody sang. Let us leave them in their uneasy dark, these shock-troops of leisure, a moment of social history fading.

1996

A Pub Cycle

I: Anthony's Quest for the Holy Ale

'AND JUST LOOK at this one.' Anthony Hackett might have been handling a plague bacillus. *La bière du Démon*. 'Beer of the Demon,' translated Hackett, peering through his reading glasses at the bearded face, not unlike his own, which leered out of the label. 'That's 12 per cent, that is, 12 per cent alcohol.' He replaced the bottle carefully among the long rows that covered the table. Screw-topped bottles, metal-topped, china-stoppered, huge green champagne-corked things, held down with what seemed to be barbed wire, deadly little brown bottles. Not one had less than 7 per cent alcohol.

'It's the lavatories that worry me,' said Hackett suddenly. 'Over there they're just cupboards in a corner of the bar; anyone can find his way out of a cupboard. Ours are up the garden. Half-a-dozen of them demons and we'd need search parties for our regulars.'

This is the story of a good man, an English publican who, fearful of what 1992 might unleash on his customers, earlier this year disappeared for four months. Now there were those who maintained he had disappeared long ago, who muttered he had only been seen twice in eight years behind his own bar, but they missed the point. Like one of Arthur's knights, Mr Hackett of the Bartholomew Arms in Blakesley, near Towcester, was on a quest.

In his cabin cruiser, accompanied by his wife, Sylvia, Hackett sailed into the canal systems of Europe to bring back the beers that will change for-ever the old habits of Middle England. For in 1992 men should for the first time in their lives know what they are drinking. No foaming agents, no anti-oxidents. No ground fish guts, onion rings or potato peelings. In short, none of the little incidentals which bring the reassuring headache in the morning. Just this one chilling statement on label after label: 'Ingredients: water, malt, hops'.

Under the huge wet skies of northern France, Hackett floated on, his boat bobbing like a cork in the wash of barges carrying a thousand Renaults. And, like Lancelot, he came on many marvels, beers of such quality, their sell-by date two whole years into the future. He found beers flavoured with real fruit ('7 per cent of strawberries and torrid pleasure'), beers made to medieval recipes, beers brewed by Trappist monks. 'Imagine the vicar running a distillery,' Hackett said.

Shady lock-keepers pressed honey on him, which he loathes, and goat's cheese, which he loathes even more, both on the unspoken premise that if he didn't buy them, the great gates might not open in his lifetime. One man got him to buy a bottle of home-made eau-de-vie. 'He made me taste it. My God. My brain went out through one ear and I found I'd given him £10.' Later he met a German doctor and warned him about the lock-keeper. The doctor asked for a taste. It wasn't dangerous, then? No, no, said the doctor, his eyes closed: it was the Mirabelle. But the lock-keeper made it in the woods, insisted Hackett. The best place, said the doctor.

Near Strasbourg he met a man who made him lace his beer with herbal bitters. 'It was unspeakably vile. I told him it was the most wonderful thing I had ever tasted,' said Hackett the European. In High Germany, his boat low in the water and clinking audibly, he had his portrait painted and sent home so his customers might not forget him or what he was up to on their behalf.

The portrait shows a youthful Hackett, the years fallen away, his beard curling like that of a Norse god. But in Blakesley the customers had an art teacher at a local school produce a replica, using the same crayons, the same coloured paper, the same frame. Only this time there were great bags under the eyes and the mouth was twisted into a sneer. When Ulysses returned to Ithaca, this thing faced him in his own bar. 'My God!' said Ulysses. 'Those four months must have aged me.'

But he had his revenge. It is autumn now; the two portraits hang side by side and Anthony Hackett has yet to open any of the bottles he brought back.

II: The Tasting of the Beers

THE MOST MOMENTOUS thing that can happen to a pub, short of closure, is a change of brew. Regulars see no reason to change their ways, so when, as happened locally in the Royal Oak at Eydon, the Watneys is taken out and replaced by Everard's Old Original, they find themselves walking politely into walls. So it was that finally Tony Hackett held a tasting to prepare his customers for what the European Union might unleash upon them.

There were five of us: Mr Blake, a driver; Mr Vaughan, an advertising man; Mr Matthews, a marketing manager; Mr Penney, a company director; and me – late twentieth-century yokels all. I had not met Mr Penney before. 'Shirts,' he said. 'Ah,' I said. Two years ago at the local fête I acquired four of his brand new shirts at 25p each, his wife having given them without his knowledge. 'They're wearing well,' I said brightly. 'Good,' he said.

Now, when they held beer tastings on the *Food and Drink* programme, Mr Oz Clarke talked dreamily about the scents of summer and that excitable blonde went pop-eyed with joy. But then they had only five bottles and sipped. We had fifty and did not sip.

'Jam,' sneered Mr Blake.

Looking back, it was a mistake to start with the Belgian fruit beers. There was poor staff work (none of us could translate *framboise*), followed by incredulity at the taste and smell. But there was a beachhead and we moved on. To Chimay. A Belgian beer, made by Trappist monks vowed equally to silence and brewing. How we laughed at this – until we drank it. 'Have you got the fire on or is it just me?' asked Mr Matthews, taking off his sweater. After Chimay, spectacles made an appearance and all the labels were read. Chimay is 8 per cent alcohol.

'Barley Wine,' muttered Mr Blake. 'Just Barley Wine and Honey.'

There was open country for a while and we moved easily among the light little lagers of France. 'Too weak,' said Mr Blake. Then the advance ground to a halt and there was much reconnaissance of Brigand, a Belgian beer. How much? Nine per cent. Good God! Like the veterans we were becoming, we settled into our trenches and waited for it to do its worst. At this point there was a long discussion on the strategy of the Gulf War, during which Mr Hackett, an old submariner, said it was up to the Navy. But it was a desert war, ventured someone, for they were his beers after all. Element of surprise, boomed Mr Hackett.

'Shouldn't touch that Brigand with a bargepole,' said Mr Matthews.

'You not only touched it, you've just drunk it.'

'Oh yes,' said Mr Matthews.

Some of the time we knew where we were. There was even a familiar brew, Kronenbourg 1664. 'Look, only 5.9 per cent,' said Mr Matthews, which was an indication of how far we had come. Another indication was Tony Hackett handing Mr Matthews a screw-top bottle to open, and, at the same time, handing him a corkscrew. But we had learned to treat a dark colour and a smell of toffee with respect. It was just that occasionally there was a ringer. *Bière du Désert*, read out a linguist. 'That means Desert Beer.' It was excellent, not sweet, and led you unsuspectingly into the desert. How much? Seven per cent. It isn't. It is. French? Yes. Typical of them to make a sneaky beer like that. So we drank Eku, an honest German brew that was exactly what it said it was, 'the Strongest Beer in the World' – 11 per cent.

'Can someone get me a bitter?' appealed Mr Blake. 'I need to remember what beer tastes like.'

There were lagers and beers dancing with sediment, which, on account of the language problem, we had shaken up. We did not drink them all, adopting the American naval strategy in the Pacific of allowing some to surrender in their own time. 'Just look at their shelf life,' marvelled Mr Hackett.

The lives we had led until this were elsewhere, so that Mr Matthews did not even bring up the subject of his recent circumcision until well after midnight. And then only in the one-act, condensed version. I walked quietly home with Mr Blake up half-known roads. There is a village in England now where men fear Europe.

III: Long Live the King

SPARE A THOUGHT for Peter Shepherd who only yesterday, a sack about his shoulders, was a solitary figure in the turnip fields of Northamptonshire, and today, at thirty-two, has more advisers than President Clinton. Old men, released from house arrest, and who never thought they would live to see the day, sink to their knees as he passes. What if a man should take it upon him to be King, mused Cromwell, but even that bold bad man shrank from this final step. Not so Mr Shepherd. Called like Cincinnatus from the plough, he has just taken over the village pub.

You who live in towns and cities will think I am joking. But then you have no idea of the power of such a man, now that the breathalyser has turned each village into a reservation. If he turns against you, goodbye social life, goodbye community, goodbye gossip. So the King is dead (or, in our case, in his long Cornish exile), long live the King.

On Day One the banned came back, like the victims of Stalin's purges – sixteen-, seventeen-, even eighteen-year men – looking around them in wonderment and wincing at the unaccustomed noise. Most, again like Stalin's victims, could not remember the youthful indiscretions that had led to their expulsion. Among them, a pale Tsarist ghost, was a man who had stormed out when the skittle alley was demolished, which no one can remember. He asked for a pint of Watney's Red Barrel, last brewed in my youth.

For something extraordinary is happening. Not only is Mr Shepherd new to the trade, he is one of us, a man many remember as a boy. On Day Two the terrible advice began. A man's life is a series of quests, most of which, if he does not wish to create too much trouble, he abandons. He realises early on he will never meet the woman of his dreams and, later, that the cost in human misery rules out the perfect state. But one quest will be with him until the day he dies. Each man seeks the perfect pub.

If you want to see what Russia was like in 1919, come to the Bartholomew Arms as the lobbies form around the new owner. First it was the Real Ale lot, to whom Mr Shepherd incautiously showed a catalogue of draught beers. 'It was a matter of "Oh, we'll have some of this" or "We'll give that a try",' he said. 'Chaps who come in once a month for a half thought it would be a good idea if I laid on nine gallons of their favourite brew.'

Then it was the Open Fire lobby, to whose blandishments he succumbed, knocking through to an old fireplace, in the process disturbing a respectable community of jackdaws and a lady in a white sweater who was having lunch when the nests came down. The fire has proved a great success, in spite of the fact that the landlord's redundant farm dogs have taken up residence around it. His wife has become so entranced by demolition she now goes around in search of other fireplaces and lost cupboards, knocking on seventeenth-century walls like a member of the Society for Psychical Research. It will take a cold, answering little voice to stop her.

In the midst of all this, as in the dawn of every new regime, the men with the large suitcases called, brewery reps unpacking their samples in front of an incredulous Mr Shepherd, who until now had not realised just how much red wine the old world had in it. He has had to resort to tastings, and listens, even more incredulously, as customers he thought he knew claim they can taste blackcurrants.

The advice is relentless, as he, and they, embark on a voyage of discovery none had known before. But there is one other thing, without which no change of regime is complete. Men who for twenty years were his predecessor's courtiers, who hung on his words, praised his tuna bake, shared his dislike of all guest beers, suddenly have nothing nice to say about him. At the Bartholomew Arms it is Year Zero again

1998

The Landlord at Bay

A PAINTING HANGS in the passageway, detailed as a *Saturday Evening Post* cover. To most people it would be the perfect pub scene, a countryman sitting in an inglenook, surrounded by gleaming brass and copper. As you look, there is something naggingly familiar about it, but it still takes time for it to register that it is *this* inglenook, *this* pub. Where have the samovars gone, and the kettles and the horse brasses?

'This feller took over. He hadn't been here a week before he'd sold the bloody lot,' said Tom O'Shea, licensee of the Old Red Lion at Litchborough. 'The week after, he sold the long-case clock and the piano an old boy had left the pub in his will.' This is the Publican's Tale.

The image is almost as old as mankind: of a well-lit room, flagstones and a fire. Nothing else at all, no piped music or lounge bar or television, just talk and the feeling that whatever has changed elsewhere, this has never changed, cannot be allowed to change. And, like his pub, the landlord seems to have been here forever; a huge man, his arms as thick as Popeye's and just as tattooed. Man and pub are outside of time and it is journey's end. Lives have been quietly given over to the quest for somewhere like this. But, as usual, nothing is what it seems. 'I'm hanging on by a thread here,' said the publican. 'When we leave I'd give this shebeen a year and a half. It's only my Army pension that allows us to carry on.'

The Countryside Agency reports that country pubs are closing at the rate of six a week, a recent survey producing the startling fact that half of all licensees did not believe they would be in business in five years' time. They blamed supermarkets and the greed of brewers who had raised the price of beer 85 per cent in ten years. There were other things, like the effect of the agricultural economy, self-assessment for tax, and the business rate. Yet for just about everyone else, such places are the stuff of dreams.

The first glimpse occurs in the collection of Welsh prose tales called the *Mabinogion*. First written down in the twelfth century, these date from a time well before that, so this is probably a description of a pub in the Dark Ages. Three men have come to a place with smoke pouring out of it. 'They could see a floor full of holes, and uneven . . . and there were branches of holly in plenty on the floor, after the cows had eaten off their tops. And they could see a dais of bare, dusty boards, and an old woman feeding the fire . . . When she felt cold she would throw a handful of husks on to the fire, so that it was not easy for any man alive to endure that smell entering his nostrils. And on the dais they could see a yellow ox-skin. And good luck would it be for the one of them whose lot it would be to get on that skin.'

Little has changed. The yellow ox-skin may have gone but the smoke still pours out of this newly lit fire, as at half-past six the cars come out of the night, disgorging council workmen, company directors and the managers of supermarkets. Had they come at four, everything would have looked wrong, the room would have been an ordinary little room they would have found hard to recognise. But at half-past six, with the fire lit and the lights on, everything is in place.

The publican is fascinated by the oddities of his customers. There is he of the inglenook, who materialises when the door opens as promptly as though he had heard the cry to prayer from the minarets. Then there is the chain-smoker with the chain-smoking wife, both of whom nightly fall asleep on a waterbed. There are now so many bicycle repair patches on it from cigarette burns that the two sleep as nervously as Judas Iscariot on his ice floe. But the publican is careful with his stories, for the publican is a public man. 'The customers have to like you. It doesn't matter how good your beer is, or your food, you and your family are in the public eye like royalty.'

A bar is the most abrupt frontier most of us will ever know, for the man that crosses it is in another country. Here he must listen to other men's woes, their views on life, their attempts at humour. Being a sergeant major in the Army, he reflected, had not really equipped him for that sort of thing.

He never thought he would end up a publican. When he was a boy in Ireland, the man who kept the pub doubled as the local undertaker. 'So the old coffin went on the slate as well.' The pub had been a police barracks, and was part shop, so small children wandered in and out. But the last time he was back, the pub was a road house in the mad new Ireland of EU grants.

He was nineteen years in the Army. 'My uncle, he was the second longest-serving soldier in the whole British Army. Cleverest man I ever knew, managed to come out a private.' He himself was not so lucky, ending up a WO (1). 'An outstanding warrant officer, a well-turned-out and smart man.' He keeps such testimonials behind the bar in a small tin box, as a shipwrecked man might keep mementoes of the old life. A slim young man in full regimentals looks out of a photograph. He was not yet eighteen when he joined the Guards. 'Three meals a day,' he said with awe. 'The spuds like boiled children, the eggs looking up at you, and all that bread. I'd never lived so well.' Which was why, when his term came to an end, he joined the Catering Corps the very next day. Food, he had decided, had a future.

It is thirty years on, and the publican the night before has cooked the annual dinner for the skittles team: for the car-dealer, the mechanic, the factory worker, the computer programmer and the salesman of dental equipment. The first course was tomato and orange soup.

'How do you make that?'

'Oh Jesus, I shouldn't be telling you such things. It was the old dodge, tinned Heinz Cream of Tomato (never any other kind), then chopped fresh oranges with orange juice. They loved it.'

Cooking in the Army was full of dodges. On exercises on the Scottish border, having been deliberately careless with their mortars, they ate sheep later the same day. After the Army, he worked for outside caterers specialising in London banquets, producing five- and six-course meals from the back of a truck outside the British Museum or Apsley House.

'But the pressure got to me in the end. I found myself just waiting for the off to get at the whisky. That was when I took this place, nine years ago. I took it sight unseen, and they were very suspicious of me at first.

They'd had four landlords in two years, and they'd heard a retired major was coming. Then one chap who'd been in the Army saw me and said, "He's no bloody major."

He came with all those odd possessions publicans bring with them, in his case pigs. Drawings of pigs, photographs of piglets, piggy banks and china pigs. He also brought his old menus, mementoes of sorbets and beef wellingtons long ago. Five-course, six-course, seven-course meals. But his recipes he threw away like Prospero, vowing he would never cook again, until one of his customers, a man then working for a catering firm, asked whether he could make use of some curry powder, his company having decided to change the constituents of theirs. The publican said yes, not thinking to ask how big the company was. The curry powder came in a pantechnicon, and the curries he has been obliged to cook, if only to get through his powder mountain, are famous. His customers have come as a big surprise to him.

But then so have his hours of work. Up at 7 a.m., he is rarely in bed before midnight. Then there is the bizarre demarcation between what is the brewery's and what is his. As a tenant, he is obliged to sell their beers and ciders, but everything else is up to him to supply. The bar he had fitted up, but a year ago the brewery bought the counter from him, making them responsible for the beer-pumps. A pub in England is, in terms of law and inventory, a place of mystery. Its fixtures and fittings, the tables, the brass that somehow survived the great sale, the sketches of long-dead regulars on the walls, he bought from the previous tenant, according to custom. Some take such things with them from pub to pub, and in time they go through many hands. It is possible that, bald and rank, the yellow ox-skin rug survives somewhere.

When he went, said the publican, he would take only the picture of his old dog.

1999

VE Day

I EXPECTED ALMOST as much of VE Day fifty years on as those of you did who celebrated it in 1945. I thought it could be the last chance for the village to act as a community. The church may still have its community, mostly the very young and the very old; the pub, even with its landlord in exile, has one, and there is also the changing community of mothers at the school gate. Apart from these, the village is as full of displaced persons as a neutral port in wartime. I expected much from VE Day.

Some worked hard to make it a success. Parish Clerk Weekley, not the power-crazed figure of my fantasies but a *Guardian* reader muttering in private that it had really been the Russians who won the war, organised an exhibition of memorabilia in the school hall. Philip Purser, formerly the TV critic of this newspaper, recorded the memories of those who had been there; he himself had reason to remember VE Day, for he had just dug a comrade's grave.

But the irony was that the picture of the village which emerged from their efforts was even more mysterious than before, for here were men I had never met, never even seen in the street, who had been code-breakers at Bletchley Park or had flown twenty-hour patrols over the Atlantic in flying boats. I walked around the hall trying to answer the quiz about the War but gave up when I found I could only answer questions I had supplied myself, such as 'What was Hitler's salary?' He made a great thing of this, for he did not take one, but this was just as fraudulent as most things about him. Hitler was a multimillionaire, living off his royalties from *Mein Kampf*, a copy of which the Nazi state presented to every married couple.

His portrait, that of the brooding man of destiny, dominated the hall, which made it look as though he were the host unavoidably detained elsewhere, like an American film star at some British awards' ceremony. As for the rest, it was amazing what people had kept, such as Ministry recipes for herring, which included advice not only on how to cook, but also on how to eat them. My wife had contributed a yellow box-kite, which pilots forced to ditch at sea would fly in the hope that this would attract rescue. She had printed her address on it.

On the playing fields a cricket match, out of the origins of the game, was being played with up to twenty-a-side, including women but not dogs. They had a barrel of beer, which might explain the rapid turnover in the batting; also the number of fielders staring stonily into space. Mrs Sylvia Hackett, wife of the exiled pub landlord, was there in the uniform of a WRN. Expansive over brandy, she told me she had always wanted to be a WRN but that her husband had never allowed it because he was one already. This fascinated me, because he is a large man with a beard.

'How did Hackett get in the WRNS, Sylvia?'

'No, no. He was in the Royal Navy.'

At one point I wandered off to see the street party and so missed the streaker. 'Very good streaking,' said an impressed Doug Blake. 'Cleared the stumps and all. At least, most of him did.'

The street party was a great success. Small children squabbled and grimly ate their way through mounds of jelly, being waited on by young women in shorts, few of whom I'd seen before, the thirty-somethings being as reclusive as mountain gorillas with company cars.

The high point of our day was to have been a sing-song in the school, together with a bar, but only forty out of a population of 400 came: 'Just enough for it to be a party,' said Philip Purser. Doug Blake popped in for a minute, looked worriedly at the wine drinkers and then bolted for the certainties of the pub. I followed, hoping to stand a veteran a drink, but they were in bed or watching television. I made do with veterans of other wars, like 'quiet, unassuming Tony Penney' as the former Marine commando introduced himself, bawling. A retired sergeant-major informed me – as he has done many times – that he had got up at half-past six every morning of his life, and I told him that he must then have left some very puzzled women all around the world. At this he stared at me in amazement, as he always does.

And then it was over. It had not been a total success, but then neither had it been a failure. When we look back on it, we will see it changed nothing but we will also remember something else: there were some who tried.

1995

Quiz Night

How is a man to cope with triumph? Disaster can be ennobling, not triumph. 'He was at his best only when the going was good,' wrote Alistair Cooke of the Duke of Windsor, and I have been brooding on this terrible indictment ever since I returned, the Eydon Village quiz team trotting at my chariot wheels. For it is autumn again, when the leaves fall and the villages compete at general knowledge.

I am not a member of our team, being a mere second reserve, but with two away they were scraping the barrel when it happened, the thing I had rehearsed in daydream. The Lord delivered Eydon into my hands. We were four, a retired schoolteacher, an engineer, my wife, who is first reserve, and myself. We had no audience, Parish Clerk Weekley, who had picked the team and brought us to the back room of the Eydon village pub, having sloped off to the bar. This reminded me of what William Wallace, at the last battle, told his doomed soldiery: 'I have brought you to the ring. Now hop.'

Our opponents certainly looked as though they knew how to hop. We were up against a college lecturer, a marketing consultant, a retired underwriter, and a lady who informed us she was retired 'from more things than she cared to remember'. Their shared experience of life seemed formidable, and so it proved. They knew the colour of an owl's egg. They knew how many people were on board Noah's Ark. One man's general knowledge, I muttered to myself, was another man's whimsy.

Of course it didn't help that, asked what the dove brought back to that blasted boat, I said 'a leaf', and was awarded *nul points* by a quizmaster whose impartiality was open to question. He later gave maximum points to one of our opponents who said the NASA shuttle had brought back that woman scientist 'from the atmosphere'. Why did she need a spacesuit then? I have held a low opinion of general knowledge ever since I lost

University Challenge for my team by declaring that Joan Sutherland and Eileen Joyce both came from New Zealand. Who cares where they came from?

Yet this is what passes for learning among the millions. When Liverpool had two graduates in that famous team in the 1970s, supporters called them Big Bamber and Little Bamber – Bamber Gascoigne, who had all the answers written out in front of him, having passed into folklore as the greatest brain in history.

General knowledge is now so much part of all our lives that without it there would be no afternoon TV, a third of all country pubs would close in winter, and village folk would know even fewer of their neighbours. Dear God, it is even a cottage industry. Near me lives the first itinerant quiz-master in the history of the countryside, a man who runs quizzes for the pubs and has a computer with 41,222 questions in it, which ensures he will not ask any of them twice in the same place. But what is general knowledge? Once, it was roughly what you would have been taught in school. But when it became mass entertainment, all that was swept aside, for contestants could not be left looking too silly.

At first in the village quizzes I was arrogant enough to get a gloomy satisfaction out of not knowing Billy J. Kramer's backing group. But even arrogance gets worn away by rounds on TV soaps, on Monty Python and, the pits, on the 'novels' of Jeffery Archer, which is why I began to dream of questions to which I alone knew the answer. And at Eydon I did.

A disgust was on our opponents' faces when we were told the name of the fictional character on whom the round would be based. Mine was the first question. 'He wore a red jersey, but there was the odd occasion when this was blue,' I said rapidly, and then watched the disgust turn to horror as they realised what they were up against.

I answered the questions my colleagues failed on; I answered the questions *they* failed on as well. I gave the name of the policeman in his village, I identified his schoolmaster, his doctor and his shopkeeper. And in all this I was just scratching at my knowledge. I could have told them who his uncles were and where they lived. I could have said where he went on holidays, named his landladies and given a quick précis of what happened to him there.

We had been neck-and-neck before, but after that one round we were fifteen points ahead and they knew they were doomed. In 1996 in Eydon they had encountered a lunatic who knew all there was to be known about Rupert Bear.

1996

The Shooting Party

THE FOG HAD not lifted, so each man in the half-circle became more and more insubstantial the further away he was; the last smeared shapes might have been scarecrows in the long fields. They stood at 50-yard intervals and were motionless. Admirers were present: a girl sat on a shooting stick beside one man, a dog crouched at the feet of another. All were in a middle ground between two stretches of woodland about 200 yards apart, and they watched the first wood so fixedly you half expected something from the Book Of Revelations to bound out at them. Had you come on the scene unexpectedly, you would have thought mankind was making a last stand here.

At first there was no sound, but then suddenly, out of the wood, there came a threshing and a breaking of sticks as though that huge creature you had imagined was being disturbed. But immediately afterwards there were sounds of unease and protest, small worried gobbles.

> They are not those who used to feed us
> When we were young – they cannot be
> These shapes that now bereave and bleed us?
> They are not those who used to feed us
> For did we then cry, they would heed us

Sometimes, the assistant gamekeeper said, he found himself wishing pheasants were not such friendly old things. He had known them when they were chicks and would come to his hand to be fed. And on frosty mornings they were so beautiful, he said, with the outrageous colour that did not belong to such a frozen landscape.

Then there was movement. Dogs squirmed excitedly, and there was click after click as guns closed and barrels came up against the sky. There were men's voices in the wood, and whistles, and then the first bird. It did not fly. It walked out of the undergrowth, an old gentleman on a morning's constitutional, looked at the guns, and at the wood beyond which would have been sanctuary, and then without hurry walked along the line of the wood out of which it had come. Someone laughed.

But then one of its cousins came, flying high in a straight line for sanctuary, as straight as the change that used to run on wires in old department stores. A gun swung and followed it but did not fire. There was a moment's puzzlement.

'Safety catch,' said a rueful voice from somewhere in the fog. Then the change was coming on wires all down the line. Kerr-akk. Thump. Kerr-akk. Thump. One moment there was something gliding, something plump, and the next there was a piece of agonised heraldry in the sky, wings extended, the feathers separate and wild. Thump. Some did not die but lay fluttering until the little yellow legs came up. One died on the edge of sanctuary as in the last reel of a war film. But not a man broke line to end the small agonies, for there were rules, and those present had always obeyed the rules.

> *If hearts can house such treachery*
> *They are not those who used to feed us*
> *When we were young – they cannot be!*

The poet Thomas Hardy was not a shooting man. He would not have appreciated that death on a winter morning is as precisely choreographed as a ballet.

It had been 9.30 a.m. when the guns assembled outside the stately home. They were not martial looking men. Most had spectacles and looked like aspirants for some safe Tory seat. Most did something in the city. And without exception they were dressed in new waxed-cotton and knickerbockers, for the killing game has its uniform. All had long, leather gun-cases. There were eight of them, young men, and each had drawn a number, for, out in the ploughed fields and meadows, sticks with these numbers were waiting for them. It was not an energetic sport, murmured their host. All day this firing squad would be driven from stick to stick, wives with them in men's hats. There were many black labradors, giving the proceedings the air of a first day at school with themselves the new boys, milling excitedly for they had not met before; the guns were prefects distant and responsible.

The beaters were off-stage at this point. They had come in a trailer, merry men more used to showing their emotions, dressed in a bewildering variety of old clothes. In jungles they would have been invisible, in the trailer they had the look of a Band-of-Hope outing; spaniels sat in their laps licking their faces. They were local men and, unlike the guns, talked with local accents. Some were farm-workers, others were from the town, drawn by the prospect of ten quid. One, a dog-trainer, had two spaniels with him; he liked this shoot because there were not that many birds. Of a neighbouring shoot with a pheasant to every shrub, he said it tended to spoil the dogs.

The gamekeeper was with them, a wild red side-whiskered man with a long scar down his cheek who would not have looked out of place cheering on the tumbrils of the French Revolution. He had a knife the size of a sword strapped to his thigh, and for this day had guarded his 6000 pheasants, fed them, patrolled the woods on damp midnights. His part-time assistant, a newsagent, dreamt aloud of the day he too might become a paid patroller of woods.

Once, he said, he came in broad daylight upon three men walking the estate with shotguns; he, hoping to add to the total of eighty foxes killed each year, had a rifle. 'And this chap, he pointed his gun at me. So I let them go. When they'd gone 50 yards and I was out of range, I put two bullets into the ground beside them. That's how I brought them in.'

But the penalties were so mild, he said, just fines of £40 and confiscation of the gun. It was the latter which hurt. But up North the law was Draconian; there they confiscated cars as well. In Scotland, though, you could be fined £100 for shooting a stag but you could also sell the stag for £500.

The host for the shoot farmed 2000 acres of arable land and had shooting rights over another 1000. He shot sixteen days a year, letting two of these out to foreigners, which brought in £15 a bird. But as it cost that to rear them, the shoot did not figure prominently in the farm accountancy. If he did away with it, would he be better off? 'Yes,' he said sharply.

On the fourteen days, the guns were either his or his brother's friends, there as their guests. At the end of the day each gun got a brace, the rest going to dealers whose phone calls began that night, each man quoting his price. In death the birds travel further than they ever do in life.

But now it was 9.30 a.m. and the guns were piling into a Land Rover like Al Capone's torpedoes off for a morning's brisk persuasion. Cars followed, with the wives and dogs, and in the rear there was a trailer pulled by a tractor. The trailer was to be the catafalque.

At their stands the guns were chatty. One said he worked for a London auction house as a gun-pusher.

'I see, you're a gun-runner.'

'No, not quite.'

After that there was a heavy silence in the fields. Number Eight was a jolly man, full of tales about Scotland. He shot every weekend in the season, he said wryly, marvelling at his own obsession. He belonged to two syndicates and also went on the odd rented day on which he could end up as one of eight splitting the £1,500 cost. He said he was a surveyor by trade; the difficulty in life was fitting in the surveying. He was not sure why he liked shooting so much; perhaps it was the feeling that came at the end of a day. Could he describe such a feeling to an Eskimo? No, he said gravely, he did not think he could describe it to an Eskimo.

The landowner's wife did not shoot. For her the day would be long, she said, if it were not for the dogs she had with her. They were there to retrieve the wounded birds that made sanctuary; it was their job to bring the soft bodies out of the wood.

'We're not doing the big woods today,' confided the assistant keeper. 'We're just mopping up the odds and ends. Why, there's one bit I know where there'd be 3000 birds in the air if we went through. That would never do.'

The beaters stood in a long line at the edge of the wood awaiting the command from red side-whiskers. It came, and twenty men climbed the wire fence. The wood was dense, brambles sprang at their faces. Once or twice there was the clatter of wings above them, an oddly hard noise. 'Watch your line,' shouted the keeper like an officer leading the toy soldiers of the eighteenth century into action. He was everywhere. 'And watch your dogs.'

No, there was no danger to the beaters, said the assistant keeper. These guns were experienced and shot high, and when it came to foreign guns the landowner kept an eye on them. In life, he said, it was best to avoid Italians. 'Hold it,' shouted the keeper suddenly, for there were gaps in the wood now and guns were going off. Then we saw what the birds had seen, the half-circle of men; we were at the wood's end, blinking in the light. A whistle went and the drive was over.

The man from the auction house owned up to having shot a woodcock. He had shot too much, he said ruefully; in his excitement (though it was hard to associate such emotion with him) he had killed young birds, not seeing the short tails in the fog. Number Eight's labrador was assembling his tally, and the two, man and dog, looked like knight and squire. He looked down at the bright feathers. Sometimes, he began, he did wish pheasants were a bit wilder, that for once they would jink or dodge.

The guns moved off to the Land Rover and lunch, and a farm-worker with a stick began tying the little bodies to this. In the trailer they were hung in rows by the neck, cocks and hens, the colours already beginning to fade. 'This is what it's all about,' said the assistant keeper without enthusiasm. 'If it wasn't for this, they say there wouldn't be any pheasants left in Britain.'

Late in the afternoon, down by the lake, we began conserving the ducks.

1991

The Village Show

THE WROUGHT IRON gate should open on the walled garden of a manor house, on avenues of trimmed box, anything but this . . . The gate opens on an allotment patch. Silver paper rustling in the wind, bamboo poles, the odd shed on a southerly slope slipping away to other villages, other spires. I thought someone had nicked the gate until I saw the inscription. 'In memory of C.H. Middleton, Horticulturist. Known to millions for his broadcasts 1886–1945.' I stared in puzzlement, as anyone under fifty would. I did not know this was a village's way of mourning its one national institution.

And it is September, when in marquees and church halls, in vestries and school gymnasiums, they are laid out like the legendary dead: parsnips creamy as ivory, thick as a man's forearm, the great carrots, the leeks as big as baseball bats, the lines of home-made wine, the fruit cakes with the patina of bees-waxed oak. It is the time of the agricultural show in England. Off-stage are old rivalries, whole days, weeks, months being given over to this moment, as all summer long men's lives have been hung up like old raincoats for the possibility of a triumph not even the Caesars knew. Triumph, plus a first prize of 40p.

In the little village of Weston most of the first prizes are 40p, except that for sloe gin, which last year suddenly was £50. And it is the first Saturday in the month, when, just as it was in Mr Middleton's day, the village show gets held. The Lord Lieutenant is opening it this year.

'Is Sir John Lowther still with us?' asks a member of the committee anxiously. The committee is meeting in the bar of the village pub.

'Absolutely,' says Francis Sitwell, lord of the manor and sometime winner of the Plate of Fruit competition. 'By the way, do remember it's Sir John Lowther KCVO, that's important.'

'Is there a full-stop between the letters?'

'No.'

The nobs have always come to the little show at Weston, near Banbury. Derek Nimmo. Roddy Llewellyn. Dame Edna Everage (twice), 'dressed up to the knockers', as Ben Jones, Hon. Sec. put it. For this was a tradition set by its founder over half a century ago when Jack Warner and Hermione Baddeley came. Nobs do, when a national institution asks them. Nobody ever called him by his Christian name, he was Mr Middleton, a man who to millions was second only to the Creator in his ability to conjure vegetables out of the ground. In a verse a little girl, asked who caused the carrots and the cabbages to be, answers firmly, 'Mr Middleton'. For some 3.5 million people listened to his broadcasts supporting the wartime 'Dig for Victory' campaign.

He was the gardener's son from Weston Hall, who, whenever he came home, was asked to dine at the Hall, an invitation never extended to his father. But by then his authority was beyond that of squires. 'This is the BBC National Programme *In Your Garden*. And here is Mr Middleton . . .' To those of you old enough these words are Sunday afternoon, and especially the voice which followed this announcement.

'Good afternoon . . .' A slight cough. 'I suppose the most difficult thing to explain over this wire is the pruning of trees . . .' It is a quick, dry voice, not that of a professional broadcaster at all. 'If in doubt, leave a tree alone . . .' It was so matter of fact: no affectations, no attempt at dramatic effect, certainly no jokes. Mr Middleton says . . .

'I remember we all had to be quiet when he was on,' said Ben Jones, a retired farmer. 'My father would come in, even though he was no gardener, just because Mr Middleton was on the wireless.'

'I think you'll find it's called the radio now, Dad,' said his son Ivor, chairman of the show for the last five years and a landscape gardener.

There is a battered paperback that still turns up at the odd jumble sale, *Mr Middleton's All Year Round Fruit and Veg* which, first published in 1944, was still selling ten years after C.H.'s death. At the bottom of every page, in heavy type, there was this rubric: Mr Middleton says . . . 'Sweep your lawn before the first mowing . . .', '. . . keep your tools clean . . .', 'there is no substitute for digging, or if there is I haven't found it'.

C.H. Middleton was from the rural working class, brought up in an estate cottage, though in his semi-autobiographical *Village Memories* he himself actually inherits Weston Hall, 'an ugly old Georgian affair with a verandah in front'. Little has changed. The Hall is still there, an ugly old Georgian affair with a verandah in front, and the marquee is up on the lawn, awaiting the public and the judging. It was his influence that started this in 1940, and it is sad to read that moment of snobbery which prompted him to dream that he was the squire's, not the gardener's, son.

He left home at seventeen. A job with a seed firm led, via Kew Gardens, to an invitation to broadcast from the BBC (and subsequently to a job on the Wartime Board of Agriculture). 'He gave added interest to life in many homes,' said his *Times* obituary patronisingly. His accent was ironed out, and it was only the odd early dropped aitch (''ap'azard') which revealed his origins. Not that he needed to bother, for the listening millions recognised him as one of their own, this man who never talked about anything but gardening. It brought him the BBC's most bizarre fan-mail, for through the post they sent in live and dead plants. He was the first English working-class hero, apart from football players and hangmen, and they felt they knew him.

'The lamentable death of Mr Middleton will be mourned by many who never felt an urge to till a garden,' his obituary in the *Observer* began.

The gate at the village allotment patch is actually his second. A national fund raised the first at the entrance to the BBC garden in Cavendish Square (now at the BBC written archive centre at Caversham). The chairman of the governors was present in 1990 when that was moved, for, whoever else they have forgotten, the BBC remembers Mr Middleton.

His niece still lives in Weston, her husband is on the show committee, and the C.H. Middleton Cup even now is awarded to the villager gaining the most points for his vegetables. The irony is that Middleton himself might never have won this. 'He did have a garden of his own,' said his niece Sheila French. 'From what I remember it was no great shakes.'

Mr Ben Jones, late of Tregaron, was talking four-foot parsnips. 'Yes, you could eat them, if you wanted to that is,' said Mr Jones. 'I don't know if you knew this, but if you want to get them that size you don't grow them in the ground. If you did you'd only get up to one or two feet.'

I stared at him in amazement. 'Where do you grow them then, outer space?'

'No, that would be against the rules,' said Mr Jones. 'You grow them in a 40-gallon drum full of compost. You make a hole down and the seeds grow straight down that. Same with carrots. Some do grow them in the ground, but not showmen. Onions you grow in the ground, so long as you keep feeding them. What with? Oh, horse's . . . you know, cow's . . . The very best, mind,' said Mr Jones dreamily. 'Couple of years old, good and rotten. No old strawy stuff.'

We talked about cheating. There was not that much incentive really, he said. When the first prize is 40p, and it has cost a man £2 to grow something, his thoughts do not easily turn to chicanery. 'Mind you, it does happen. We had an incident thirty years ago, the man's dead and gone, it was over onions, and we had this rule we could inspect the garden. Well, as it turned out, he did have onions in his garden. But we still don't know whether he growed 'em.'

Cauliflowers were tricky. One of their judges, a Wappenham man, insisted he had seen one of the entries that morning on a grocer's van, but again, how could you prove it? They changed the rules after that. Cauliflowers now need a *stem* at the Weston show.

Oh yes, there had been some legends among the competitors, like Lewis Blencoe, ninety years old and still competing. One year Mr Blencoe had twenty entries in the Silverstone show held the same afternoon, and also competed at Weston. But the old showmen, father and son agreed, were beginning to drift away. 'We tried a novice class for the youngsters,' said Ben Jones. 'That didn't work. I don't know what'll happen in the future. We got the women in, doing cakes and chutneys. Then we had a cooking class for men. 'Course, we don't know whether their cakes are ready-made or not.'

And what happens to the entries? They got eaten ('except for them bloody parsnips, that is'). Even the wines got drunk, usually by the committee if the competitor had not claimed them. One year they got through the lot. 'Real good stuff,' said Ben Jones. Amongst the entries there was parsnip wine, 20 per cent alcohol by volume. 'Powerful bloody stuff,' said Ivor Jones. Elsie Hatton said her husband, Doug Hatton, the show chairman, had been making wines for thirty years. 'He even made the wine for our wedding, we couldn't afford anything else.' The sad thing is that Mr Hatton, a fork lift operator, is now diabetic, and their house, said Mrs Hatton, was filling up with wine.

The roles change, the faces do not. In photographs of past years there is Ivor Jones, then chairman, presenting Doug Hatton and his father with their prizes. All look extremely surprised, as though these meetings in the marquee were the first time they had set eyes on each other.

But now it is 1998. The marquee has been booked (at £1,500, with tables), the caterers contacted (for there will be the usual dinner, at £10 a head). What about a short-fall? Some 600 people usually came, at £2 a head, and they just about broke even, I was told. They owned various things in the village, like the five-acre allotment patch, all of which helped.

The committee was meeting in the local pub. Would the WI lay on the teas as usual? The WI had not replied as yet. Were they going to advertise in the local paper? Advertisements were expensive, said someone. 'We have to pay for something,' said Ivor Jones. 'You have to speculate to accumulate.'

They worried about sideshows. Mr French said he had heard of a man who grew orchids and, it was agreed, he should get in touch with him. They had had a fuchsia grower, said someone, and he had been a great success, only he just came the once, disappearing in a blaze of blooms.

Mr Sitwell from the Hall arrived, who had been responsible for bringing the show back into its grounds (his father, Sir Sacheverell, had not been that interested in gardening). Mr Sitwell provides the wines and has often carried off a 40p first prize. 'Mixed fruits,' said Mr Sitwell. 'Always mixed fruits.'

There were talked about past shows. Frank Wills remembered 'them shallots twelve years ago, as had already beaten me at Cropredy, only they was under another name there'. And then there was the matter of the new category, sloe gin, with its remarkable first prize. I quote in some amazement from last year's programme: '*First prize, £50. Second, 30p.*

Third, 20p.' That, they said mysteriously, was because they had a sponsor for sloe gin, but nobody seemed inclined to say more. They even had someone prepared to judge it. 'We shall have to lay on a supply of biscuits for him,' said a committee member. 'Also water,' said somebody else. So they ordered another round of drinks, and Mr Hatton the chairman said, 'Do we need another meeting?'

'Oh yes,' said the entire committee as one man.

1998

The Fête

I HAD KNOWN THE day would come. It was just that I did not think it would come so soon. The lady said, 'I think you'll regret this,' as she handed the package over. The prize-winner's small fist closed round it, there was the sound of tearing paper, and at the tombola stall my daughter, aged six, had her hands on her first bottle of nail varnish.

It is June in England and on greens and glebe fields, in gardens embarrassed with summer, in aid of church roofs, scout troops, PTAs and the unfortunate who are offstage, the village fêtes are being held. From drawers and cupboards where they had lain unopened and unwanted, they now lay in lines on trestle tables: soaps that relieve you of most of the external symptoms of the Black Death, bottles of alcohol-free wine (there is *always* alcohol-free wine), bottles of hair highlights with the mad-lipped faces of forty years ago on them and gift-wrapped talcum powder from long-forgotten Christmases.

The matrons who preside over these horrors are as insistent as gully-gully men. The vicar hovers benignly so that I have to turn away as I pick up *The Intimate Memoirs of Dame Jenny Everleigh*, a paperback which has on its cover a lady in her underwear but wearing a hat and gloves. '1op,' says a grandmother. 'They're all 1op.' I point out that twenty years ago such a book would have landed her and me in a magistrates' court. 'In that case,' she says, '2op.'

Tell me where all lost books are. They are all here, the forgotten, the unfashionable, the loopy, all 1op: *The Thoughts of Chairman Mao*, the strictures of Dr Leavis, the memoirs of Sir Philip Gibbs, the poems of Whittier, and a book on marriage that nowadays would read like a car manual but here includes a chapter on etiquette. I pick up a biography of Coleridge costing less than chewing gum and read of his attempts to start a magazine. This foundered when he carried an article on fasting under the headline: 'Wherefore my Bowels shall sound like an Harp.'

I find his daughter's memories of the poet Yeats who, hard of hearing and getting his first wireless, leant forward politely to address it, 'I beg your pardon.' Later he became addicted to cowboy fiction and, delirious with illness, called out to his wife, 'George, George, call the sheriff.' But also on stall after village stall, a reminder of what is to come, the massed baleful paperbacks of Mr Jeffery Archer.

The afternoon moves on. A brass band plays. A beautiful teenage girl, with the light down on her upper lip that would have had Guy de Maupassant (who loved moustaches on women) rattling the bars of his short stories, is attempting the sort of exercise the damned will have in hell. She is slowly, so slowly, passing a metal loop along the twists and turns of electrified wiring. When it touches this a bell rings. Crouched over the thing, the down glistening with sweat, she is almost there . . . when the bell rings. She immediately starts again.

The smell of burnt sausages drifts over the honeysuckle. I pass the jumble stall and resist the temptation to buy back my old Portuguese Army shirt. Ah, but a much older friend has gone, the shirt with the rhinestone poppers. Vanity of vanities, says the preacher . . .

And now the exotic ones have arrived, scrupulously scruffy from immaculate period houses where from Monday to Thursday the lights do not come on at night: the weekenders are here, who talk only to each other, of dinner parties gone or to come.

Three o'clock, the puppet show is over and it is time for the painting of the children's faces. They wait in line for the creams and the chalk, my daughter among them, so that when I go home a thing in warpaint pads beside me, still clutching the nail varnish.

Much later on the stairs I hear this: 'Thank you God for my nice day and for the nice time I had with the nail varnish. Please bless Mummy and Daddy . . . and the varnish. Please help me to be good and to put the nail varnish on well.'

In the lamplight the clasped fingers are gleaming to the first knuckle.

1989

Hymns Ancient and Modemed

AT JUST AFTER 11 o'clock two policemen call, and, as they stand
there in the farmyard, it is clear from their faces in the light of two
hurricane lamps that for them the twentieth century is ebbing. Through
the open doors of the barn they are peering in at an England that was
already old when their great-grandparents were young.

But at least the policemen have got in. Fred Huggins, who runs the bar,
was once asked by a man if he needed help. Fred mentioned pay. 'I don't
want pay,' said the man. 'I just want to get in. I've been trying for the last
four years.'

It is not the entrance fee; that is just £9 for the three days. Nor is it
geography, for the farm is almost exactly in the middle of England, a few
miles from the M1. It is just that those who come, 150 of them, to park
their caravans and put up their tents, have been coming for the past fourteen years, so whatever else this is, it is a reunion, and nobody comes to
watch.

It is a matter of a top hat. The hat hangs on a rafter in a barn, and hat
and barn have both seen better days. But when the hat is taken down, whoever holds it sings, and everyone who turns up will in turn sing, the others
joining in the chorus. There are no song sheets, even though in the course
of the weekend 450 songs will be sung. There is no musical accompani-
ment either. Between songs they will drink 150 gallons of beer, these
huge men, some with beards halfway down their chests. As for the
women, no one in his right mind would pick a quarrel with them.

What each does for a living, the rest do not know, for nobody asks.
Jobs are elsewhere for these three days, being part of that twentieth century in which nobody, it is thought, can possibly hold the words of 450
songs in his head. Some of these songs are centuries old, some the singers
have written themselves. There are love songs and drinking songs, songs

the soldiers sang in the Great War, negro spirituals, work chants, music-hall songs, songs in dialect about events long ago. And some of them are funny; some so beautiful that Mr Huggins at the bar is crying into his change.

There has been no rehearsal, yet the blend of voices is so perfect you cannot believe you are hearing it here in this dusty place. But then some of these performers would head a bill elsewhere, being professional or semi-professional singers. They do not need amplifiers, some you could hear fields away, so there are none. Or stages. Or stars. For this is not entertainment as you or I know it. This is entertainment before the inventions of the twentieth century relentlessly turned us all into an audience. Before television, before record-players, before radio; this was how men sang in pubs and at harvest suppers.

'The old people would recognise some of the songs but I think they'd be startled by the intensity,' said Tom Brown who, with his wife Barbara, organises the Song and Ale at Whittlebury. They hold it here because once they happened to meet the farmer. Tom works for Wandsworth Borough Council and I know this because I asked him.

'I'd rather be a beggar than a king,' belts out a man from Milton Keynes, who then stops. 'Not in that bloody key I wouldn't.' He is an environmental health officer, which would come as a shock to the others who know him only as the author of a song on the last great whale.

When his daughter left home, a man tells me, he took early retirement, sold his house and now he and his wife travel the country in a camper van, seeing the places they always wanted to see, doing the things they wanted to do. For them this weekend is a fixture.

There are no songs about merry England, no self-conscious folkery. One man alone does not sing: a Lancashire poet, his voice, I am assured, was so dreadful that when the organisers wanted to raise a collection, the threat that he would sing was enough to have money dropping into a bucket.

Near the close there is an extraordinary moment. On their 40th wedding anniversary a man starts to sing 'My Old Dutch' to his wife but stops when he realises he does not know the words. There is consternation, for in this gathering, incredibly, nobody else does either. But twenty minutes later the man stands again and completes the song.

Someone here, at midnight, in a farmyard in the middle of England, has tapped into the Internet to get the words. For this is 1997, after all.

1997

PART EIGHT

COUNTRY MATTERS

Stubble-Burning in the Home

THE MOST EXTRAORDINARY case I have ever heard of has just ended. A twenty-nine-year-old sheep farmer, living in a village just 5 miles from where I am writing this, pleaded guilty to charges of threatening women over the telephone until they agreed to set fire to their pubic hair. The extraordinary part is that the women frequently did.

I first became aware that something very odd was going on when last year our local giveaway newspaper printed a police warning to beware of some anonymous caller making what were described as 'perverted suggestions'. No details were given and nobody I talked to had even heard of it, but, by then intrigued, I rang the police and the full story emerged. The calls were being made during the day, always during office hours, which suggested to the police that whoever was making them had access to a firm's telephones. Because there were so many calls, with some lasting up to half an hour and often much longer, they thought no one around here could afford the phone bill.

The form the calls took was this: if a man answered, the caller immediately rang off, but if it was a woman, he then engaged her in conversation. He did not make threats at first, he just asked them about themselves. The police said he extracted information from them 'like a practised journalist', which showed a touching faith in the powers of practised journalists. On some occasions he already knew something about his victims from local press items or wedding announcements, but much of the time he just found out about them from what they told him. For these women talked to a stranger.

Now in the country you get used to being rung up by strangers; every week some woman I have never met will ring to ask after my windows or kitchen cupboards. They sound so concerned, their vision of an ideal home so precise that I listen to them with interest, for nothing much happens here in the days. By nine in the morning the villages are empty of everyone except the old, the unemployed and young women at home with their children. The caller knew how vulnerable his victims were.

The young women were bored and lonely, so of course they talked to this friendly voice and, incredibly, told him about their families. It was then that the threats started. At first he claimed to have kidnapped their children, was torturing them and would stop only if ransom demands were met. No money was ever delivered (apparently he asked for thousands of pounds), but then in April last year the threats changed, when he began to demand that they set fire to their pubic hair.

Now the extraordinary thing is that they believed his threats. They wouldn't have done so twenty years ago when a village was a place where you knew your neighbours and your mother lived just down the road, so a lunatic on the telephone would have been a joke over the garden fence. But they are vulnerable now: they sit at home, listening to the news bulletin reports of kidnaps and urban terror on the radio, and are afraid.

You see the fear in village streets where no children play and cars deliver them to their friends' homes, as though an English village in the late twentieth century were downtown Detroit. Nobody questions this. Nobody has ever heard of a child being taken, yet we listen to the news on which such things happen and assume it is only a matter of time before it happens in our village. The only crimes around here are drunken driving and the theft of slates from barns out in the fields. There is little else, apart from the odd burglary, and even then half the village has a fair idea who has been responsible. Once there was a murder, but that was in 1873 and the murderer was arrested an hour later. The one thing which has changed is fear.

This may take a ludicrous form, as when after the Libyan bombings Gaddafi was briefly as much part of rural demonology as Napoleon had been and some old people refused to open their doors. A young man in black leathers taking photographs of houses in our village had his motor-cycle number taken by just about everyone who saw him, until it turned out he was on a location shoot for *Country Life*. Against this background, young women in the spring of 1991 began setting fire to their pubic hair.

Nobody knows how many did. The court evidence mentions twelve cases, but these, as the police admit, were the only ones reported to them; others may have been too embarrassed to come forward. In evidence, a husband reported returning from work to find his wife naked and trembling, still holding the telephone.

When I first started talking about the pubic hair burning, it was suggested that all this had occurred only in my own demented imagination, and I almost came to believe this, for I heard nothing more about it. Even in the village pub nobody knew anything, and when I brought the matter up the barmaid dropped a glass and said I would be none the worse for some medical attention. But then there it was again in the giveaway paper, but this time as a front-page headline: 'Pervert jailed for sick calls'. He got five years. The police, who had hoped to catch him on his phone bill alone (350 reported calls were made), did so in the end only when a man took the receiver from his wife and recognised the voice.

A plump, red, grinning face looked out of the newspaper photographs, the sort of face you can see any night of the year in the pubs of middle England. His defending counsel, describing him as 'a friendly, likable and highly respectable member of the farming community', said his client had made the calls because at the time he was under severe financial pressure.

Oh, dear. Even in its economics this case will tell you as much as you will ever need to know about life in the English countryside in 1992.

1992

Lost Knowledge

I**T IS A WET** Sunday afternoon and I am being shown the one thing on which all human history turns. It is not the wheel. It is not the stirrup. It is not the compass or the clock, being far more important than all these, for this ensured our survival as we inched our way north into these latitudes. I am being shown an apple.

Not just one apple, but a line the length of a cricket pitch laid out on the tables in the marquee, apples I have never seen before and which the supermarkets never will. Huge red footballs, the result of God knows how many mutations, are beside tiny dawn apples, and there are apples that taste of pineapple, and the dour russets Shakespeare knew, for he compared Falstaff's nose to one.

And Barry Juniper (now there's a name for folklore), of Oxford University, is warming to his theme, which is not the long march of everyman, but the long imperial march of the pippin which made that possible. The apple was the one source of vitamin C it was possible to store, moving out along the Old Silk Road from central Asia, the home of all apples. I can see them in furs, moving north, little groups of men and animals after the Ice Age, munching on that one item without which, in those long winters, they would have perished within two or three weeks.

There was no need of horticulture, as man, donkeys and horses have no gizzards, and the apple seeds passed undamaged through them. The result was that so relentless was the march of the pippin, so infinite its capacity for mutation, that by the late nineteenth century every town, even every village, in central and southern England had its own local species of apple. But then Mr Juniper stops his version of world history. 'You know, I practically have to drag undergraduates out to the orchard.

If it's not two-and-a-half inches across and wrapped in polythene, they don't recognise an apple. This is the Tesco generation . . .'

A bush grows in Milton Keynes. It is in a public garden in the centre, and the blackberries on it gleam in the sunlight, lush as plums and enough to keep a bakery in full production for a day, but nobody picks these black-berries, although thousands pass. And there is worse. In the village of Newnham, in Northamptonshire, there is a nuttery, two to three acres of it, looked after by the Woodland Trust and open to the public, who may pick the cobnuts for free. These hang in clusters, avenue upon avenue, and it takes me about ten minutes to pick two or three pounds. It is like har-vesting the Garden of Eden.

Mr Juniper of Oxford tells me that cobs are so rich in protein and oils that a man could survive on a diet of just them and apples. But the only other living things I have seen in the Newnham nuttery are half-a-dozen squirrels, too fat to climb, who amble up and down between the avenues and eat the fallers. I know people eat nuts, for two miles away Waitrose stocks them at £1.50 a pound, brought by road from Kent. They even eat those half-rotten Spanish things, buffed up at Christmas to conceal their age. It is just that they do not pick them.

Nobody picks anything now, and if moments of social history intrigue you, put down this. Nature has become as dangerous and as alien as any landscape in which Captain Kirk and the crew of the Starship Enterprise ever found themselves. Two generations ago, children in the countryside still walked, munching, along the lanes to school, as they did in *Lark Rise to Candleford*. But to their grandchildren the hedgerows, once larder and pharmacy, are an anonymous green frieze.

We forget the names of things, then we forget their uses, and finally we become frightened of them. A friend told me how an old gipsy had rec-ommended a yearly purge of bracken fronds, a whole panful cooked in butter. Who would dare to eat that now? First we feared the forest floor and its fungi, then we feared the hedgerows, and finally the trees.

Who picks elderflower now? At any country show the saddest exhibit is the forlorn little cluster of wines, for while the carrots get bigger and the cakes glossier, the winemakers dwindle, so sometimes you find that one man has won every prize, there being no other entrants. Yet I have tasted elderflower wine as subtle as any Muscat.

You will not find the lost knowledge of mankind in a Himalayan monastery. You will find it in a country lane, and it was lost, not long ago, but in your time.

1996

The Walk

THE WOOD, as usual, was a compromise. There are more things than one man may turn into a wood for, ventured the poet Edward Thomas. So true, squire, so very true. 'You two may do just what you like,' said my wife. 'I *need* to go for a walk.' And so we did, all three, muttering and distracted like a peasant army of the Middle Ages.

According to my wife, when a man marries above him there is always some piece of grit in the eye. For me, this grit is the walk. My family walked because they had to, they walked to market, or, in my mother's case, the five miles to school, until, aged six, she ran home when she met an otter. When the car came, all walking stopped. But my wife's family, who already had cars, did not. They just walk and, with some large dim dog for company, would be happy on a treadmill.

First, we row about walking, then, having accepted there is to be a walk, there is an abrupt switch to the particular: where is it to take place? I like towns late on a Saturday afternoon when I can haggle over the loose grapes and the fish. My wife likes green places with no people in them – it is such a shame she was unable to follow the Black Death round old England. Still, there it is, no go the beauty spots, no go the vistas, and it is time for barbed wire again and the 'goodness, what a very unpleasant notice'. And we are off to the woods.

Amazing places, woods: they represent or have represented absolute privilege and absolute licence, and both at the same time. I don't know if it comes from some race memory of the Norman Forest Laws, when a chap like me could be flayed alive for making a deer pant, or from having read too many crime stories in newspapers, but I feel anything could happen to me in the woods. On this occasion we had agreed we would go into what remained of the forest of Whittlewood, part of the old Royal hunting reserves when these covered a third of England. It was out of this wood that the young King Edward IV burst, thirsty and randy, to marry the first widow who said no and thus prolong the Wars of the Roses by twenty years.

We had to drive there, another bone of contention, as my wife expects a dream wood to start at our gates, but then all squabbling stopped. We found ourselves passing one of the saddest places on earth, a modern deer farm. With its high wire fencing and great aluminium gates, this could have been a Nazi death-camp under the trees. All herd instinct had gone, so the inmates did not bunch or even look up as we peered in, but went on grazing listlessly in ones or twos. God knows how you would have made any of these pant in the short time before the abattoir lorry came.

We had stopped once before this, only to find the screen of ash concealed the eldritch gloom of conifer trees, once of interest to accountants when they had a tax advantage, now of interest only to the Admiral, whose conifers in our village, according to my neighbour Douglas Blake, will soon be so high they will require aviation warning lights.

We parked finally when we began seeing pools of bluebells, which reminded me of a girl photographer I knew who was commissioned by a calendar to do a tasteful series of nudity in a wood. The bluebells, she told me, had been a terrible nuisance, being so small and cold they got everywhere, and her models could not stop giggling. But I kept that story to myself.

Have you noticed how sound dies in a wood at the first snap of a broken branch underfoot? The bird song which at first was so insistent was immediately further away and even the gobble of the cock pheasant dwindled. But then you might just as well take a Chieftain tank into a wood as have an eight-year-old girl with you. 'Mummy, we had this jumble sale at school.' I could hear the clear insistent voice 30 yards away. 'And the word Deutschland came into my head. That's an odd word, isn't it, mummy?'

There was a scrabbling of claws as a squirrel burst out of a hollow oak, burnt out inside so that five men could have stood up in the black interior, and clearly dying, though the branches didn't know this, for there were green leaves bursting out of them. 'A rotten tree lives only in its rind . . .'

I remembered this from Robert Graves's poem on the Roman Empire, when emperors came and went but the frontiers held because the men there also didn't know this.

'Deutschland is Germany in the German language . . .' In a shaft of sunlight a hare loped soundlessly and was gone, and, watching it go, I saw a pair of black knickers in the dead leaves. Ah, country matters. But I moved them with my shoe, saw they were ripped across, and there was an ugliness in the wood.

'I don't think I can spell Deutschland, mummy.' It is nice to be eight and to have a mind that moves on rails.

1991

The Red Field

IN THE BEGINNING there was the green field; and how long ago that seems, now that the countryside looks like a vast Impressionist painting. We had just become used to the yellow fields of rape when the blue fields came – the blue of a linseed crop, which on a hillside looks eerily as though a lake is cascading down. And this year there is the red field.

I saw it when I was driving westward at sunset. There was a mass of yellow next to it, a crop of late rape, and there were green hedges around, but inside these was this bank of red, of poppies. But who grows a crop of poppies? I knew that in the quiet villages of West Wales graduates supplemented the good life by growing cannabis, yet something on this scale had to be beyond the ambition of everyone except the cocaine cartels of Colombia. In Northamptonshire?

I am walking the footpath through the west of the county which has been named the Knightley Way. The irony of this will become apparent. I have started among lawns like green baize and bunkers of sand where there should not be sand; I am crossing Farthingstone Golf Course and it is a moment to reflect that within the next ten years all Middle England could look like this, when the golf courses now being opened join up.

Then there is the first field, a frontier as abrupt as that in a fairytale, with a sign telling golfers not to venture further. Squirrels flow out of the barley as we approach, for it has been a good year for squirrels. We cross a road and suddenly are on land that has been looked after. An old cyclist told me once that in solitary confinement in a German POW camp he had kept sane by letting the roads of England unroll in his mind. You could tell then where Gloucestershire ended, he said, and Oxfordshire began because of a difference in the materials used for roads. The same is still true of farms.

You come to a hedge where all the gates swing true and no binder twine secures them. And it is like that here. These gates have been replaced in oak and, through the field of rape below us, the land falling away in terraces, a footpath runs like a hair parting. Yet here, to the left, is the field of poppies. What is even stranger is that a firebreak has been created at the edges so the flowers are massed in a small space like an eighteenth-century army.

We walk down to Snorscomb, which is where the irony intrudes that this path should have been called the Knightley Way. You will see a sign at the crossroads pointing to Snorscomb, only there is no Snorscomb. There was once, when this was a village, but the Knightley family closed it down in the late Middle Ages, as they had closed other villages, to make sheep pasture. I climb the slope of the field where the village was and see the long depression of what must have been the main street. A hare with one ear up and one down watches me from the grass. The Knightleys were actually done for this in the 1520s because the Crown had become worried at the number of beggars being produced from these closures. Not that it worried the Knightleys, for the fine was a trifling one and they went their merry way. When the eighteenth-century enclosures came, a Knightley asked if he might sow a last crop on land destined for some villages; he sowed oak, ash and elm. A descendant, trying to evict a tenant, had his roof taken off at night.

Now all that remains of Snorscomb is a large farm by that name. Some old brothers lived there when we first went by, and the outbuildings and house looked in need of repair. Then two years ago the new gates appeared, so it was clear a new owner had come. But as we walk past the yard now, all repairs have stopped, and there is a sign outside the house giving warning of its state. Later I learn of the tragedy that has overcome it. An industrial tycoon bought the farm from the brothers, spent money like water and was then killed in a riding accident. The farm was subsequently bought by a company.

We walk on and come to the allotment fields of one of the most beautiful villages in England, Everdon, under the hills. I used to know a Romanian chap who until his death two years ago was intent on building up the first allotment empire here; he had six plots and used a tractor. It is early evening now, when the Spirit of Night has come over the Western

Ways to open all the little pubs, and there is that lovely sound of English summer, a dozen hands clapping raggedly at a village cricket match.

And the Red Field? There is a clue in the cleared strip around the poppies which suggests a field a farmer has been encouraged to forget, helped by £80 an acre.

In a few years there will be no mystery, when up to 30 per cent of the Eastern Midlands could be under Set-Aside. This first Red Field is how the future will look.

The Secrets of the Pond

THE VILLAGE HAS suddenly become very interested in its old fish ponds. Something has to be done about them. For in winter they flood, the water spreads across the road and the council has to come with pumps. The place looks so terrible – a half-acre of mud, fallen trees and undergrowth, the perfect setting for a horror film, with something rising out of the slime. Only the odd cat goes there now; the ponds are too filthy even for small boys. Yet the old men remember fishing there, and being chased away.

There were two ponds, an upper and a lower, dating back to the Middle Ages, but, with the passing of the last squire, nobody in the village took an interest any more.

For the fish had died when someone tried to clean the ponds and disturbed the sludge, so that the upper drained into the lower pond. The older inhabitants remember the expiring roach being laid out in rows. And now it has been suggested that they be made into a small park. If that goes ahead, it will mean a lot of work; it could also mean some very startled workmen . . .

Jack was on leave when he heard the planes overhead, coming very low, but it was late in the war and he took no notice until he heard a muffled thud, as though a door had slammed in the earth. When he got outside he saw smoke rising about two miles away. Two American bombers had touched in mid-air, and one, a Flying Fortress, had crashed. When he got there Jack was very frightened because a petrol tank had fallen into the lane and the fuel was everywhere.

In a field he saw a huge tall section, sheered off and complete, and, round it scattered like seeds, was the gleaming brass of cannon shells. The young men had not had a chance, and their bodies were scattered across miles, in woods and fields. One they did not find until months later when the kale was cut. The country people had had a terrible shock. Still the years passed and they forgot.

Until, that is, not very long ago when a woman, recently widowed, asked Jack to call on her. She had found something very odd in her husband's shed. When Jack got there he found himself staring at more brass than he had ever seen in his life, shelf after shelf of it, row upon row, neatly stacked and gleaming. Cannon shells quietly gathered, brought home, and even more quietly polished among the seedlings and the mole traps until the brass work was as bright as the day they were made. But what was to be done with them? They couldn't put them in a bin, and nobody could want them back, not after all those years. The police would just ask questions.

So late at night, spade in hand and a sack on his back, Jack set out for the one place he thought no one would ever use again, a place he knew well from his own childhood. Deep under the mud of the old fish ponds, Jack buried the cannon shells.

1987

Wildlife

A HUNDRED YEARS AGO, almost to the month, a railway company mislaid a passenger. The telegram, on a London & North Western form, is dated 10 July 1887 and is signed by 'Allen, Rugby'. Whoever he was, Mr Allen did not waste words. 'TIGER ESCAPED FROM 9.42 P.M. EX-BROAD STREET TO LIVERPOOL BETWEEN WOLVERTON AND RUGBY STOP WHEN FOUND FORWARD TO LIVERPOOL STOP IF FOUND REPLY.' Now read that again. 'When found forward to Liverpool.' Just that.

As far as he was concerned, it might have been a Jack Russell which had gone missing – not 600lb of carnivore stalking the Midlands at night. They were giants, our ancestors. A Mr Thomas Coleman was also distantly interested, for on the back of the form he wrote: 'Seen between Blisworth and Weedon. Blisworth said not caught at 6 a.m.' Perhaps the tiger never was. Perhaps it just roamed the Midlands forever, knocking off the odd sheep or curate – articles in which the Victorian shires abounded and would never miss – for there were no more telegrams.

I mention the tiger because I believe in the wildlife of England the way people once believed in fairies. They must all be out there somewhere in the hedgerows: polecats, stoats, probably even the odd wolf. It is just that I don't see them. I read country columnists who have badgers call on them as assiduously as double-glazing salesmen, but in thirty years I have seen just three badgers; all were dead after traffic accidents.

And I watch natural history programmes on television to find myself flying wing-tip to wing-tip with wild geese. Or I'm a ptarmigan, suddenly freezing into the undergrowth as a terrible shadow blots out the sun and an eagle sails overhead.

All this has a bad effect, for photography has reached such perfection now that the real world you yourself see afterwards cannot compete and has a faded quality, like advertisements in the windows of failing shops. As

Dylan Thomas wrote about a nature poet: he had seen the country only once, from a train window, and it had looked a bit unreal to him.

The country, I had started to believe, was something which happened to other people. Until, that is, my wife opened a hostel for battered hedgehogs. She puts out milk every night and watches discreetly from behind curtains as they grunt their way towards it. Once, she added the remains of a parrot fish, which an ambitious local supermarket imports from the Seychelles. It would be the first time in the history of the Earth, she said, that a hedgehog had ever eaten parrot fish. The next morning the fish was there again. 'That was the first time a hedgehog was ever sick on parrot fish,' said my wife, proudly.

We, too, are acquiring a place in the scheme of things.

1987

PART NINE

RECORDERS

Nightmare in Lark Rise

IT WAS SUCH a small house, one up, one down, and so oddly situated at the end of a track, facing away from the rest of the hamlet that, a former resident noted, it seemed about to run away into the fields. Nine years ago the Sparrowhawk family moved in and became invisible.

'We had a plumber in, and my husband was in the bedroom with him when a man walked up the stairs. Now this stranger is standing there, *in our bedroom*, and he says in a loud voice, "Surely they didn't sleep that many in this one room." The plumber had such a fright,' said Susan Sparrowhawk. And that was just the beginning. A whole theatre company came up their drive, talking in even louder voices, and completely ignored the watching Sparrowhawks. People came with cameras and took pictures, so the family took pictures back in the hope this might embarrass them, but it had no effect at all. Think about this for a moment. As far as the outside world was concerned, the Sparrowhawks could have been holograms or ghosts – *in their own house*. But it was another ghost the world had come to see.

One hundred years ago Flora Thompson lived here. She called the hamlet Lark Rise, though its name is Juniper Hill. But the Sparrowhawks had not even read *Lark Rise to Candleford* when they came; they bought the house because of the acre of garden that went with it. They knew of Flora, for there was a sign on their wall, 'Flora Thompson, 1876–1947, Authoress, lived here', but it was a small sign, as self-effacing as Flora herself. They had no idea of what she had to come to mean for so many, but they were to find out.

There are some people who can ignore the past when they acquire it as a lodger. They sell the pulpit where the great man preached, plough the meadow where a battle changed the course of history, and paper the room where a murder took place (or, in the case of one hard-riding horsewoman in west Wales, simply do not bother; the blood was on her wall years later). But it is different when it is not the past but you yourself who becomes the lodger.

Flora Thompson was born Flora Timms in the cottage now known as Lark Rise, though in her time that was the name of a field, for fields had names then. I remember when the cottage came on to the market fifteen years ago. I was having a drink in the village pub, which closed this year, and I asked what the price was: £50,000. £50,000 for a one-bedroom cottage with a bit tacked on? They nodded gloomily. That other cottage, Queeny's, just in front of it, said the landlord, had fetched £35,000. So why the extra £15,000? 'Literature.'

The irony is that the fame that came with the publication of *Lark Rise to Candleford* as one book (previously it had been three) came too late to mean much to Flora. 'Twenty years ago I should have been beside myself with joy, but I am now too old.' She died two years later, a retired postmaster's wife in Devon, and her passing did not make the *Dictionary of National Biography*.

She would be amused by her reputation now, for the people who read her and come to Juniper Hill do so for the glimpse of a Golden Age, the old lost life in the English countryside. But Flora Thompson was writing about a society in ruin. Their traditions may have gone back a long way, but these were the poorest of the poor, their rights to the common land, to graze their cattle upon it and collect firewood, having been taken away from them in living memory. They barely survived here, nursing their half pints in the pub, singing songs which had been handed down and which they no longer understood. This is the idyll of Juniper.

Someone with a sense of humour called it a hill, for it is so low it is even below the line of the main Oxford road, and passing trucks are strung out against the skyline. The hamlet began as a huddle of squatters' huts on the common. When the common became enclosed, the tiny houses drew even closer together, like animals before a storm, for they were now lost in a sea of agriculture and other men's property. The hamlet, Flora's father said, was a spot God made from the leftovers of creation. But now it is so sleek, many gardens bursting with blossom and one of them with the efforts of a landscape gardener, his sign left proudly on the gate. Juniper Hill, its pub gone, is a dormitory village. She did not know her neighbours, said Susan Sparrowhawk, they came and went so quickly.

Susan Sparrowhawk of Lark Rise . . . she feels herself so engulfed by ornithology that when in a hospital waiting room a nurse called out 'Susan Pigeon', she automatically stood up. Her husband Kelvin is a sales manager; they have three children and two bedrooms. 'I didn't mind the people coming at first. I'd say, "If you want to look, do come in." But then I got irritated because it was clear they felt they had a right to come. We put new windows in, but I walked behind a group of people up my own drive and I heard one say, "Surely they can't do that." You've no idea the trouble we've had trying to make this place habitable.'

They have, in fact, been told by their local planning officers that they cannot make any more alterations, and the fact they had two elderly Minis in their drive brought the council conservation officer and the chairman of the parish council to protest. But the Minis are still in the drive. 'The way we look at it is that it may be *her* history, but it is *our* house,' said Mrs Sparrowhawk.

Marjorie Goodings, the previous owner, once came back to find people having a picnic under her apple trees. 'Another time I came out, hearing voices. And there was this woman in my garden telling another one where the pig-sty had been. She seemed to know where everything had been. But she didn't even look at me.'

The pilgrims visit four sites: the Cottage, the church at Cottisford and the Old School there, to which Flora walked across the fields, and then the Post Office at Fringford a few miles away, where she worked; Fringford she called Castleford.

Flora's father – the stone mason who came down in the world, and drank – is in Cottisford churchyard, and on a brass plaque fixed to the wall of the church is the name of her beloved younger brother Edmund. At school she protected him, but there he is, killed in the Great War with ten others 'In the cause of Right', his name, E Timms, the last of all. The visitors' book is full of his sister's name now. 'Following Flora Thompson.' 'Admirer of Flora Thompson.'

But even these diehard fans would find it hard to identify the Old School where Flora described the infants chanting their alphabet ('Once started, they were like a watch wound up and went on alone for hours'). Fourteen years ago when this was up for sale, the estate agents chorused, 'Reknowned [*sic*] for its mention in the autobiographical volumes published by Flora Thompson.' But when it comes on the market next there will probably be no mention of Flora.

The present owner has carried out a conversion so complete that the Old School would not look out of place in Beverly Hills, with its latticed dormer windows, double garage, conservatory, 10-foot-high conifer hedge and the hacienda-type wall – a building out of time altogether. It is the wonder of the area that this extraordinary confection sailed through planning restrictions while the Sparrowhawks' application for an extra bedroom was refused.

A sleekness has fallen like snow on these villages, and when I stopped to buy eggs at Cottisford, I found the vendor playing tennis on her own court. The Post Office at Fringford closed so long ago that nobody even knew where it had been and I found myself directed to two different houses. Flora would have found it very odd. 'To be born in poverty,' she wrote not long before she died, 'is a terrible handicap to a writer. I often say to myself that it has taken one lifetime for me to prepare to make a start. If human life lasted 200 years, I might accomplish something.'

Yet this is where it began for her, the little girl who kept her secrets (it took her teachers a long time to find out she could read). Beyond lay the other villages in the south of England and the husband who thought her writing a waste of time. Only three photographs were ever taken of that thin face which gave nothing away.

And now strangers come, hoping to find a landscape in which time has stopped. Only time never stops. The Sparrowhawks have put a sign on their gate – 'Keep Out. Private Property' – more in an attempt to reassure themselves than anything else. It is such a wistful little sign.

1997

The Village Historian

IT IS WHEN THEY talk about change that the old stop you in your tracks. A gentleman of ninety-five once solemnly informed me the biggest change in his long life had been the fact that ocean liners now had rope ladders leading down to swimming pools where previously they had steps. Mr Reggie Chapman, eighty-seven, said it was the quiet, which in his old age had settled on the village like snow.

Poets burble about a lost peace, but not countrymen. Mr Chapman, a silvery, whispering gentleman, very bent ('like Nebuchadnezzar, I am almost down to the grass'), remembers the hullabaloo of his youth in Abthorpe, near Towcester: the church bells, the school bell, the sound of children playing and of cows being driven back into the village at night. He has seen them all go. The last vicar went in 1943 (on the advice of the diocesan lawyer, who thought a new vicarage roof would be too expensive). The school closed in 1959; the main employer, a shoe factory, had closed in 1936; and one by one the farmhouses slipped into the excited prose of estate agents ('genuine period, scope for conversion . . .'). So Mr Chapman, finding himself in the time of greatest change since the Enclosures, wrote it all down in a book.

Now many old gentlemen are moved to do this, and their pamphlets crowd the shelves behind the cash desks of whatever bookshops survive in market towns. But Reggie didn't write a pamphlet; he didn't even write a paperback. He sold his lace collection and his silver to publish privately a history the size of a family Bible.

These I Have Loved comes in an edition limited to 500 copies. It costs £40 and weighs five. 'I doubt whether any other village has something this size,' murmured Reggie. He typed it all himself. 'I did it because I wanted to do it. I've recorded everything, the clergy, the schoolmasters, and it's all there. I wouldn't care if I sold only twenty copies and had to burn the rest. It's done.'

He was only ever out of Abthorpe for three years, when his parents pushed him into a bank in Yorkshire. His health broke down and he returned to keep chickens, then the post office, but mainly to keep an eye on everything. He is unmarried. 'I'd have made a better gypsy than anything else,' he said, not wholly convincingly. 'Just an old illiterate who collected things.'

Which he did – charters, old law suits, family trees – so much that Reggie is the most controversial man in the village, and of the fifty-five who have so far bought his book, some have done so by night. I live not far away and have heard many stories, most to do with local misgivings about the use to which he may have put his considerable knowledge of the past.

It is always disturbing when a man turns out to know more about your grandmother than you do yourself. 'It is quite terrifying what he knows,' said one villager. 'I was having trouble with some people who, he told me, were all illegitimate, while the grandfather was a well-known lunatic.' He was also able to range at will through history. When the church was trying to raise money for a new roof, Reggie emerged to tell them of the body to which the sixteenth-century power of patronage had passed; the roof was paid for. 'If the village weren't so sleepy, it would have known,' said Reggie. Selflessly he looked after the village reading room for them, but somehow ended up owning it, for he sold it: the village woke up then.

He has also owned many houses, including the one in which I sit writing this. How did he come by them? Villagers who tolerate absentee landlords mutter when one of their own is an astute businessman, and what made it worse was that he kept his own counsel in the dark thatched house beside the green. A Catholic convert, he was always a man apart.

Thus much of the book is taken up with his theory that Abthorpe always quietly adhered to the Old Faith in all but name. Protestant bogey figures like Henry VIII's torturers bound into these pages, while Queen Mary's enthusiastic barbecues go unrecorded. Shakespeare, said Reggie, was a Papist.

And from time to time the curtains lift on little private lives, like that of the courting couple overheard when past a point of no return. 'Do yer love me, Bill?' It is an anxious voice, and there is a pause. 'Do yer really love me?' Then a strangled, cross voice. 'Lub yer, lub yer, course I lub yer. I lub yer so much I could gnaw yer bloody ears off.' Then the gentleman in chapel, concerned about draughts, hissing, 'Wind, wind', to which an old lady replies, 'Don't be such a fool, man, us ull be all right when the organ starts.'

In that room beyond the low porch, where little has changed since before the Great War, among landscapes in dark oils and heavily floral wallpaper, the piano and the old photographs, the long thin fingers have typed, recording it all. And it is done.

1993

The Painter

YOU ARE IN THAT south-western corner of Northamptonshire which one man has caught so perfectly, so obsessively, in oils and watercolour, that if you live there you begin to suspect the existence of a vast wooden frame below the horizon. You are in the world of Peter Newcombe.

I know his lanes, his water meadows, his churches, and have seen his flare of light, which comes abruptly around 4 p.m. in autumn like a spotlight from the western sky. Or rather, I have been made to recognise them from paintings that an old lady once told him made her cry. Here are the little barns in the fields which most of you have seen from a car at some time or other, in ruins now, for farmers no longer winter their cows when rustlers have lorries. Yet these footnotes to a farming past he makes things of wonder, standing out of the corn or with ploughed autumn earth breaking against them.

The stone pillars and thatch of the oldest barns. The leaning wooden posts and corrugated iron of the poorest. And then the most bizarre, blue bricks and red, the white stone and herringbone tiles, row after extravagant row, as the old brickies showed off in the fields, far from disapproving architects. Look, the painter is saying, there are little palaces out there, there is arch after perfect Moorish arch. You have only to stop – only of course you never do stop. But he did.

Newcombe was brought up in this world. He is fifty-four now, the son of a carpenter and grandson of a shepherd, who until a few years ago still lived in Blisworth, the village where he was born and which, apart from a year at art school, he did not leave until he moved six miles away into the farmhouse he has spent the past twenty years, not converting, but ushering back to its origins as a seventeenth-century manor house. He was briefly the village postman but for the rest of his adult life has been that rare thing: a professional English artist.

The result, as he acknowledges, is that he has become a source of wonder among local people. 'It's the fact that anyone can make money by painting; it always comes back to money with them. One old chap asked me, "You ain't got a picture for my boy Billy, have yer? A che'p on', what'll go for more next year?" I met him again after an exhibition. I was in his fields watching the harvest. "'Ow did the show go then?" He saw my new car. "Ah. I can see how the bugger went."'

The irony is that Newcombe himself sounds just like the farmer at times. In his current exhibition there is a painting of an old wooden cart, of which he told me once, 'Bought that cart for £40. Painted it so many times I can't remember, but I got £1,500 for one of them.' This is a man who was once employed to clean out a barn used by circus elephants as winter quarters. He was cleaning out stuff, he said, which was as solid as peat and as aromatic as pipe tobacco. He can point to the tidemark on a barn wall and tell you it is that height 'cos one year the spring was so late the muck reached higher and higher before it could be spread on the fields. Yet this is someone whose living turns on the prices his paintings fetch in galleries he rarely visits.

So he has become a man apart in his world, which may be why he has emptied it of people. There are none in his paintings. 'I do look at people, but then it is usually as interesting things. I like the old, I think I relate them to trees, but I don't have much curiosity about people. If I meet someone I might ask him what he does, but then usually I say "goodbye".'

He was always a man out of his time, as he found when he did a teaching diploma at Bournemouth. 'I tried hard to find things to like about Bournemouth. Ever so difficult, that. I was writing essays about education and it became an endurance test.'

He returned to Blisworth where, to the alarm of his parents, he became the postman, doing his rounds in the morning and painting in the afternoon. In 1967 came a turning point in his life: he found a copy of *The Shepherd's Calendar* by the Northamptonshire poet John Clare.

'And for the first time I had found someone who thought the same way as I did, who just observed things, and I couldn't get over this bloke who liked the things I liked. I just had to illustrate it. I did twelve drawings. It

took me a month to do each one, propped up against the piano at home.'
The drawings were exhibited at Northampton Art Gallery and shown on
television. Later that year Newcombe made his first visit to a London
gallery, the Furneaux in Wimbledon. 'I took this load of work up . . .' He
made it sound as though he was delivering logs. 'The man saw them and
said, "We'll take you." He didn't say "we'll write" or "we'll ring". I was
over the moon. It's the big thing, the entry into London.'

It was then that Michael Shepherd, the former art critic of the *Sunday
Telegraph*, saw his work. Shepherd recalls, 'I remember saying to myself,
"this chap has something to say, and has seen something". D.H. Lawrence
once said, "All art that is worthwhile has a gleam of a place."' After that the
world called. He painted three Shell calendars in six years and did that
series of British flowers postage stamps many of you will remember. So
started the most remarkable lifestyle I have encountered in late twentieth-
century England.

He paints every weekday from 9.30 in the morning until 9.30 at night,
and this year everything he has painted has been within walking distance of
his house. At weekends he works on the house. He has built his own stud
walls of plaster and oak, replaced beams, carved an entire room in lace
panelling and ripped out grates to expose the hearths of the past. Every
building craft has been learned and mastered: joinery, plumbing, masonry.
For there is no rush in his world. What was a year, he asked me once, and
answered his own question: a year was nothing. But then there are no
deadlines, no colleagues, no bureaucracy. He paints what he wants, when
he wants, where he wants.

And at 9.30 at night he drives to a country pub where he drinks one
pint of beer with his girlfriend, who works in a solicitor's office in a nearby
town. You could tell the clock by him, a neighbour said once. He is indifferent to food, to any form of social life, and to travel, though once a year
he goes on a week's holiday to Dorset. So it has been, so it will always be.

'I can sit in a field for a month and not be bored. See that windmill? I've
painted that in winter, I've painted it in sunlight. I painted it once with a
fox sunbathing under a hawthorn tree and 10 yards away there was a
pheasant doing the same thing. But animals don't bother you. People do.

Their dogs leap up, they try to talk to you. I remember this chap when I was sitting on the towpath near Stoke Bruerne, painting the locks. "Mind if I look?" I ignored him. He said it again. I still ignored him. The next thing was, he was kneeling in front of me, looking up my nose. "I'm really annoying you, aren't I?"'

If you are unused to him, he can sound like a visitor to this planet, about some business that has nothing to do with mankind. 'I sit there, the loneliest person in the countryside, yet they have to come up to me.' And what they don't interrupt they destroy. Lowndes Barn, near his home, he loved ('a concoction of lichen, asbestos and rusty tin, all held together by orange tile ridges – a gift for any artist'), but it was pulled down nine years ago.

Still, there is something worse than destruction. 'One week I go by and the old roof is off, but the next week a chimney is there. Someone is converting it into a house.' The result is that he is painting more and more in an environment where no change comes, like the three fields he himself owns, where the foxgloves grow, the bindweed and buttercups, white violets and dog roses, all that inventory of wildflowers that elsewhere the sprays have killed. 'Sometimes something hits you between the eyes and you have to get down what you see. See the toadstool in that painting? The sunlight hit it like a floodlight. It wasn't there yesterday, and tomorrow it won't be there again. But, just for a little while, it was.'

Here no ambulance crews stop, seeing him in a ditch, to ask if he is all right. No policemen knock on his window on the premise that anyone who sits all day in a car must be on drugs. He is going to keep things like this.

1996

PART TEN

WHAT MIGHT
HAVE BEEN

Byzantium on the Great Central

U P THERE, MOVE to the parapet and, apart from the fear when you see the cattle below are like toy animals, all that registers is that where you are is a marvel of engineering. But from below, looking up at the perfect arches of brick thrown into air, you are conscious only of beauty. In Northamptonshire you are in Byzantium.

Byzantium is just five miles from where I live. When I was there in the heatwave, I saw a golden oriole, the rarest of visiting birds, and another time a fox appeared from nowhere, barking irritably, for they do not fear men here, and grass has grown over the carriageways of the highway in the sky. The Great Central, of which this viaduct at Helmdon was part, was designed 100 years ago to be the most perfect railway ever built. From Sheffield to Marylebone its stations were so neat you cannot believe what you are seeing in the old photographs. And as for its gradients . . . there were none. The railway cut through every hill and was carried over every valley. One minute, as you walk the old line, you find yourself ringed by sky, then ten minutes later you are in a place of shadow, the cutting is so deep and the indifference to geography of those long dead engineers so absolute. Barbara Castle closed the line thirty years ago.

And geography is at last having its revenge, for I have reached a stretch that could be in the Amazon Basin. I am deep in mud, ragwort and hogweed towering over me, and I am having to remind myself that the anaconda is not indigenous to Northamptonshire. In two miles I have gone from sky to shadow to swamp. But at least I know where I am. I have met people who remember trains on this line, but what will our children make of it, and their children? A time will come when they stare at this viaduct the way the first English invaders stared at the ruin of Roman Britain, and like them think it the work of unknown giants.

There are eight stations in this county where once there were eighty-three, when the rails went everywhere. From the Great Central I am looking down on an earth embankment which carried the Stratford and Midland Junction trains on a line so slow that one driver carried a shotgun in his cab and blazed away as he passed, stopping if he bagged anything. The bookings clerk at Wappenham, though on duty, went gathering watercress, fell in the river, and in his guilt and confusion hung his clothes around the station stove while he, behind his tiny window, dispensed tickets all afternoon naked in the steam.

I am passing Moreton Pinkney now. Sixty years ago there was a lady travelling to this village from Byfield four miles away; it took her two days. A clerk put her on the wrong train, so she went up the line to Woodford two miles away. They sent her back but by then the last train had gone. They offered her a bicycle, which she refused. They tried to hire a horse and cart but none was available, so in the end they found her rooms for the night, where, shaken by her experiences, she locked her door. In the morning neither she nor the station staff could unlock it, so they put a ladder against her window, down which she came to complete the journey she could have walked in an hour. But a railway ticket she had bought and a railway journey she made. On my left is the station where she alighted, a farmyard now, where someone once lit the fires, punched tickets, invoiced the rabbits, blackcurrants, straw and mushrooms sent up the line. It must have been like garrison duty on the fringes of a dying empire.

Past Moreton Pinkney, and the Great Central, again a highway in the sky, is one last sagging set of signals. The rabbits tumble out of every bush. But then abruptly the highway stops, for below Eydon, the bridge is down. Yet even here the old grandeur survives, for it was not enough just to build a bridge. They built a curving wall of brick up to it topped by decorated coping, so now in its ruin this looks like the entrance to some great fortress, Alesia on the hill, where the Gauls made their last stand against Caesar.

But we are slipping on cinders now, and a teenage girl is protesting with the concentrated indignation only teenagers can achieve that she should have been brought to such a desolate place.

1997

Still Waiting for Napoleon

I T WAS NOT, said the estate agent, like selling a house. Houses he knew about, and warehouses and shops. His firm had even sold off airfields and old army training grounds, but not anything like this. This, he said thoughtfully, was a 'one-off', as he peered at the gigantic outlines of what might have been. In all the long and remarkable history of his calling, it had never before fallen to an estate agent to sell a place where his country intended to make its last stand.

Early in the new year the firm of Hillier Parker of Grosvenor Street, London, is inviting tenders for 32 acres of Northamptonshire. They are acting for the British Government, which, after exactly 180 years, is finally leaving Weedon, and a name which has lurked longer and more mysteriously than any other in the footnotes of history is now in a sale prospectus.

Few of you will have heard of Weedon. If you have ever driven through it (usually because the M1, four miles away, is undergoing yet more repairs), you may retain a picture of a slightly fly-blown village with a crossroads, a clutch of antique shops, some pubs. But had history taken a different turn, there is not one of us who would not have heard of Weedon. Hastings would have been an obscure skirmish beside it; and there would, of course, have been no Waterloo. For it was here that the British king and his government planned to stand at bay had Napoleon come, as he was expected to, in 1803.

Let us play amateur strategists for a moment. Take out a map of England and find Weedon, on the A5 just north of Towcester, and what do you see? First, no location in England could be further from the sea: it would have been the epicentre of resistance to a naval invasion. Now look more closely. Watling Street, the Roman road, or the A5 as it is called, runs through Weedon, and crosses the Saxon Portway, the A45. The

Grand Union Canal runs through the village, next to the main railway line north. The M1 is just a few miles away. Engineer after engineer, a line stretching back through Stephenson to his bustling Roman predecessors, appreciated the significance of Weedon: it straddles all routes north through the Watford Gap. Even today, with a squadron of tanks and a few surface-to-air missiles, you could cut England in two at Weedon.

But in 1803 strategy turned on the canal. Mud and the weather would have done for Watling Street some months of the year, but the canal was the military highway (as late as 1824 a convoy of twenty-eight boats went through, taking troops to Ireland). And in 1803 Parliament voted £100,000 a year 'for erecting buildings for the service of His Majesty's Ordnance' at Weedon. What the act did not say, and which emerged subsequently as tradition and in a strange little letter written by Queen Victoria, is that Weedon had also been earmarked as a retreat for royalty in case of invasion.

Even now when you look down from the hills you are aware of something very odd: eight huge red buildings, each the size of a country house, strung along a hillside, dwarfing the rest of the village. It is even odder when you walk through Weedon and in a high wall come on a lovely yellow brick pavilion over a massive portcullis, barring the way to what remains of the cutting from the canal. The elegance is startling enough but the size is out of proportion with everything around. Through the bars of the portcullis you see long wharves ending in a second pavilion.

It was this portcullis, and the two beyond it, which would have been winched down at the first flash of bayonets in the valley of the Nene. Behind it they would have waited, old George III and his fat sons, all debts and adulteries forgotten; and Mr Pitt with the biggest cache of port wine ever assembled in one place, awaiting Napoleon's coming. They would have watched those hills for the first sight of the plain blue coat amidst the gold braid of his staff. But of course he never looked down on Weedon. 'I am not saying that he will not come,' the old Admiral St Vincent had rumbled. 'All I am saying is that he will not come by sea.' Napoleon did not come.

One hundred and eighty years later Richard Ashworth of Hillier Parker was speculating as to possible buyers. 'I think someone who has created an empire in his own lifetime could well be interested,' said Mr Ashworth innocently. The royal family never did come either, though it was some time before it forgot Weedon. There is a curious paragraph in one of Queen Victoria's letters where she mentions that William IV was warned of the dangers of national rebellion if the Reform Act was not passed. 'He replied that if it did bring about a rebellion he did not care; he should defend London and raise the Royal Standard at Weedon . . . and the Duchess of Kent and the Princess Victoria might come in if they could.'

Desolation hangs over Weedon today. There are weeds in the blocked-off cutting, and rubbish and old boxes bobbing under the portcullis. The gates are open and there are no guards. But even in living memory it was not like this. Dick Denny, who has worked here for twenty-four years, remembers when the gates were shut, when loose talk in a pub could cost a man his job; when, in the great brick buildings, greased rifles were stacked to the eaves. For over a century and a half this was the most important military establishment in the country and its main arsenal.

In 1831, with revolutionary scares persisting, batteries for cannons were built on the hills and a regiment of the line stationed here on permanent garrison duty. 'A large quantity of bedsteads, bedding and barrack furniture' had passed through the gates, noted the *Northampton Mercury*. A year later, when an act to establish a railway line from London to Birmingham was held up in the House of Lords, one question secured its passage. Would it, enquired their lordships, pass near Weedon? It would. Stephenson and his engineers, foreseeing this, had swung the line in a wide detour from their original survey.

But the nicest thing about Weedon was the way it stayed resolutely in the footnotes. Not only was it the most important single place in the kingdom in terms of security and strategy, it was also potentially the most dangerous. Guns and gunpowder came by canal as late as 1882, but the cutting crossed the railway, and both canal and railway were at the same level: a section of the busiest railway line in Britain had to be pulled up each time a barge entered the depot. There were hundreds of trains hurtling through each day, and the magazine contained 1000 tons of gunpowder. Had a train fallen on a barge, it would have made Northamptonshire one vast smoking crater.

A similar dottiness surrounded the road, which at that time crossed a wooden swing bridge that had to be opened when the barges came. Miss Lillian Partridge, who has been a clerk at Weedon since 1953, remembers being taken as a child to see the bridge open, which was done once a year to enforce the army's right. Armed troops were present and the portcullis was winched up. This remains in good working order, though the canal cutting now goes nowhere. In a room empty except for twenty-year-old newspapers, the machinery is still tested, though no barges and no enemies come. The clock, installed in 1814, still beats the quarter-hours over the village. It is one man's job to keep both clock and portcullis working.

Weedon's importance persisted for most of the twentieth century, and with it those little flurries of comedy which were always in the margins. In 1930 the Army Bicycle Section transferred there, so it became the Central Ordnance Depot for Small Arms, Machine Guns and Bicycles. From 1922 to 1938 it housed the Army Equitation School, training men for the cavalry wars which never came. But in just thirteen months during World War II, from October 1942 to November 1943, 3.5 million rifles were issued from Weedon.

The end came fast. In 1961 stores were moved to Donnington (in Operation Nettlerash) and in 1965 the flag was lowered. Sixty acres were auctioned off, most of them to a wholesale grocer, and the Equitation Centre pulled down. But there still remained the central buildings, all eight of them Grade Two listed as being of historic interest. These passed to the Government's Property Services Agency, and Weedon entered the most curious stage of its career.

Watering cans, said Ken Allen, Superintendent of Weedon: dustbins, mops, ash trays, crockery, candles. Candles? Emergency lighting, said Mr Allen solemnly. How many candles? Mr Allen said he did not know, such details being kept on a computer in Hastings, but there was one vast magazine building full of candles. He was certain, said Mr Allen, that it would have been quite possible to issue every single British civil servant with a candle from Weedon. And for a moment the image came of those wary millions stretching over the hills, candles in hand. Weedon became the biggest broom cupboard in British history. It still stores all the domestic equipment that the government will ever require in any part of the earth: crates for the Falklands, crates for the Seychelles, crates for Nepal: all of them packed and waiting in the vast Georgian halls. All are to be emptied, candles and files dispersed, in what could be the greatest clean out in the history of the civil service. It is hoped to sell Weedon as a single site.

The winds were howling as we walked round, and the massed reeds hissing in the canal. Mr Allen unlocked armoured door after armoured door in their towering arches. One building was crammed full of old Inland Revenue forms, shelf after shelf, miles of Cellophaned indices, with a dead pigeon on the stairs and pools of water where the rain had come in. Yes, Mr Allen said, the Inland Revenue had been known to come here to consult its files.

In a corner of what had been the most closely guarded place in Britain even up until thirteen years ago, someone seemed to have built himself a smallholding with ducks and chickens and dogs and cats. There was also a 40-foot Ferro-concrete cabin cruiser nearing completion, propped up and almost ready to enter a canal which went nowhere. Perhaps some civil servant was planning a Viking funeral for himself or a life in the sun on his pension. How he would get the boat out was another mystery.

Forty people are employed at Weedon, of whom just six will keep their jobs and be transferred with the scouring powder and the mops. Once there were 700 civilians here. The effect on the village, said Miss Partridge, would be a catastrophe, a small catastrophe in terms of statistics, but here, in this place, absolute. The estate agents walked to their car with the aerial coloured photographs they had commissioned. He would, they told Mr Allen, be seeing a lot of them in the next few months.

It was getting dark and there were people moving among the wharves. For a moment you could imagine them: the ghosts of those who had not come to Weedon – royalty and revolutionaries. But it was the end of the afternoon shift, past the platform to which no rails run, past the wharves from which nothing leaves. The clock struck, keeping its perfect time.

1985

The Aviator

A BARLEY MOON is rising, so bright you do not notice the things below it, like this obelisk in the fields of Northamptonshire where a young man fell out of the sky one September afternoon in 1899. You do not even know his name, which so easily might have become one no schoolboy forgot. For a moment look up at what might have been, for something is crossing that moon.

His name was Percy Pilcher, he was thirty-two, and at various times had been, not the character in musical comedy his name suggests, but a naval officer, a lecturer at Glasgow University, and finally an engineer who invented the first internal combustion engine small enough to be carried in a flying machine. Only reports now survive of the lost engine with which an Englishman might have made the first flight years before the Wright Brothers.

In the last crowded minutes before the curtain rose on powered flight, inventors were broadly divided into two camps: those who thought sheer power could blast men into the skies (Maxim had two steam engines built, developing 300 horsepower in a 104-foot span biplane); and those who believed aerial balance should be achieved first. Percy started as one of the latter, a gliding man.

He had had four gliders, or soaring machines as he called them: canvas and bamboo structures tugged into the air by horses and, once, by a boy. But there was a fifth. This was already complete, together with its four-horsepower petrol engine, when Percy made his last flight. It was a tragedy of good manners. Cap on head, trousers tucked into long woollen stockings, Percy, a pale, clean-shaven, earnest man who reminded contemporaries of a vicar, was the perfect Boys' Own hero. A friend, as you might expect, of Baden Powell, he described himself as 'gentleman' in his various patents.

In the years before 1899, he had already made four gliding flights of up to 400 yards at altitudes of between 20 and 50 feet. That September afternoon he was at Stanford Hall near Rugby, the home of his friend Lord Braye who, however flat his ancestral acres, still had enough horses to get Percy airborne. Other friends had also turned up, Baden Powell among them, and it was for them that Percy, ever the gentleman, decided to make the attempt.

He must have known he should not have gone up that day, for it had rained and the rain had shrunk the canvas, putting a strain on the fuselage of his glider. But he did go up and was at 30 feet when one of the guy ropes parted, and his machine, controlled only by movements of his body, began to describe a forward somersault in the air. The wings folded and he fell to earth where he lay, the wreckage of his plane settling around him. He did not regain consciousness.

It might have become the British Kittyhawk, this corner of the Midlands, where in a few weeks only the farmers will come, the impatient sweeps in the earth showing where they tug their tractors around an obelisk that has no business in a 20-acre field. But step through the looking glass. Above you, against the barley moon, Percy is flying.

1995

The Lost Village

MOST WEEKENDS from now until the end of summer, small groups of people will trudge up some rising ground to stare at a field of wheat near Kettering. The farmer's wife has got so used to them, she feels she should lay on cream teas, were it not for one thing. She has still to get used to their reaction. 'They look at the field, then turn and look accusingly at us. And some of them, they appear so nonplussed, they go away shaking their heads.'

The reason is that there is nothing there. Yet, on the Ordnance Survey, footpaths converge and the name is in the typeface given to villages; it is there again on the roadsign at the junction below you. But follow any of these to Faxton and there is no village of Faxton.

That still does not explain people's reactions. There are an estimated 3000 deserted villages in England, over eighty of them in Northamptonshire. Those who visit these do not glower at the man in the tractor passing over forgotten main streets. But Faxton is different. Faxton is unique. What happened there happened in living memory.

It would be wonderful if we could trundle on some villain whom they also remember, like Colonel Loader, the squire who almost did for nearby Maidwell. Loader was a plant collector whose only interest in his village was to drape creepers on the houses. There was nothing you could do except stay indoors like Sleeping Beauty, as the undergrowth slowly shut out the sun. Until the roofs fell in, that is. At which point you had to move out from the rainforest of Middle England.

But at Faxton there were no villains. It was just too small and too remote, though 150 years ago there were 108 people in twenty-two houses. So the roads never came, or the piped water or electricity. It was a place from which people walked away. My friend George Freeston's cousin was the last person born there, in 1907, so his childhood was as lonely and as poignant as that of the crippled boy left behind in Hamelin. He carved walking sticks and made cricket bats, though there was never anyone to play cricket with. What is even more extraordinary is that in the 1920s the people of a village, just 10 miles from Northampton could have been living on the frontier of the Old West. On soggy winter nights they lost their way home from market and could be heard shouting out in the fields, so the dogs were made to bark and guide them in. They lived mainly on rabbit, and the shopping was communal – orders ranging from women's combinations to pig food, all bought once a week in Kettering.

This was a religious service at Faxton: 'There would only be my mother and myself, sometimes; occasionally my father would help swell the congregation. The Revd Watkins-Pitchford took the service, played the organ and took the collection as well. Sometimes I rang the bell, sometimes he did.' Only a single pillar is left now. The church was pulled down in 1959, some of the wall plaques are in the V&A in London, and the pillar behind its fringe of young aspens out in the wheatfield looks like some sinister pagan memorial. The only wall standing above two feet is that of the last house, from which the last inhabitant went in the 1950s. The only complete building is her privy.

And now people are back. They stare reproachfully from their cars, having never known the loneliness and the poverty which once was village life everywhere. The farmhouse was built after everyone had gone, yet someone surely must be guilty for what happened here. After all, nobody can blame this one on the Black Death.

1990

PART ELEVEN

INTRUSIONS

Icarus

I MET ICARUS last week. He was pacing up and down among the corn-stalks, looking very sorry for himself. 'The blooming weather changed,' brooded Icarus. 'We're coming down all over the bloody place.' His glider, slewed to one side and with one wing tip up and one down in the field, looked as disconsolate as its pilot.

The clouds had thinned and risen ('Large cumulus to altocumulus,' whispered my daughter, relentlessly), so there were suddenly no upcur-rents of warm air, and out of the bland, blue sky he had fallen. 'I was on my way to Husbands Bosworth,' said Icarus, making this sound like Samarkand.

The late Sir Peter Scott once told me that there was one good thing about being a TV personality: it allowed you to land your glider in a corn-field. 'You get out, and there's this chap waving his arms. "I say, I say, you there. What d'you think you're up to . . .? Hey, aren't you . . .? Yes, you are! Listen, are you all right? Why don't we pop over to the farm for a coffee?"'

Icarus had been lucky. He had seen from the air that the corn had been cut in the 20-acre field, so he was able to use the stubble to cushion his landing. But the extraordinary thing was that a craft weighing 5 cwt had come down without leaving any sort of impression on the ground. I said to him that gliders would be ideal things for spies to use. 'Ideal, if you've got four more spies on the ground to help you get airborne again,' muttered Icarus, refusing to look on the bright side of anything.

It has always fascinated me, this idea of turning up in a strange land-scape, that standby for thriller writers like John Buchan. A man falls from a train, floats down on a parachute, wades ashore through the marshes like the wretched German spies who turned up on the Norfolk coast wearing spats during the last War, thinking these were English country clothing; they hanged them. How long would it be before you found your bearings?

It happened to me once when I went up in a balloon, and the winds carried us over Bath, three men in what one of them was acutely aware was a laundry basket at 2000 feet. Sounds travel upwards, and even at that height we could hear people in the streets below. But then the winds swept us on again, so what had been intended as a short afternoon hop turned into an ascent of five or six hours. On and on we went, over fields too small to land in, over hedgerows out of which rabbits came tumbling, for the effect on animals of the balloon's shadow was amazing. Cows ran, pigs skidded in the mud, a Jack Russell went round and round an old man. I could hear him shouting, 'What ails you, you little bugger?'

The other two in the basket were in training for a world record hot air balloon ascent, so they were wearing parachutes. I didn't have a parachute, and it was remarkable how much this rankled the longer we drifted, and I watched the night come on. At one point an aircraft materialised and flew large puzzled circles all round us. In the end we landed on some common. 'For God's sake, don't jump,' I was told. 'If you do we'll go up like a rocket.' As I privately considered them responsible for everything that had happened, I fought down the impulse to jump, then everything was collapsing around us, the canopy and the basket, which turned over. There were two crashes and then we were down.

We had not a clue where we were, but a chap who had watched the huge boiled sweet descend turned up from somewhere in a Land Rover. I went up to him and asked, 'Is there a pub?' Not, *where* is the pub; *is* there a pub. Little lights were on all round the bar. The brass was gleaming. And there was never a pub like this in the history of the world, which was always full of pubs (there were 160 in just one part of Pompeii). I drank three pints of beer in ten minutes and rejoined the human race, which appeared glad to see me back. I had no interest in what happened to the balloon.

Icarus, on the other hand, having paid £5,000 for his glider, had walked to the nearest farm and phoned. The car and trailer took an hour to come. 'I wonder, could you hold that wing up?' he said to me. 'I should tell you, as soon as I pull this bolt, it's going to become heavy, very heavy.' He pulled the bolt, the wing came down on me and the fuselage lurched on to its side with an ugly crunching sound. 'Shit, there goes the wireless,' said Icarus. 'Oh, sorry, I didn't see you there,' he said to my wife.

I liked Icarus. A tall, blond, rueful man in shorts, he was in what was to him the middle of nowhere, on his first flight across country, his glider in pieces, and there he was distributing apologies all round the field. Later he started to laugh.

1992

The Probe

THE PROBE HAS been withdrawn, which for three months has hov-
ered over the village relaying information back to the alien
intelligence that sent it. And what was its leave-taking, some glint of metal
high in the setting sun as the gods called their chariot home? No, it was not
quite like that. There was a snap of clipboard and a hitch to a mauve ski-
suit. The alien intelligence, in this case the Professor of Geography at St
David's University College, Lampeter, investigating 'the nature of rural life
in Britain', had found out all it wanted to know, and the blonde from the
National Opinion Polls was gone.

One household in six in the village was questioned, but apart from
them nobody knew about it. And they said nothing to the rest, which
should tell the Professor more about rural life in the 1990s than any of
their answers. Twenty years ago the village would have been buzzing.

As it was, we should just have been a place name in an index with
quotes attributed to socio-economic categories were it not for one thing.
The last interview was with George at the post office, and George
thought it would be a laugh if I sat in on it. Who's this, then? He's my
agent. Alas, National Opinion Polls would not agree. I was allowed to
talk to the researcher but only between interviews, so it was a sort of
ringside chat. A good girl, Harry, but I could see she was going in the
4th.

After three months the researcher was so groggy with information that
she was beginning to forget who had said what and when, but on the
whole people seemed to be happy in the country, she said brightly. Why?
The fresh air. No, she had not met anyone who did the sort of things
people are supposed to do in the country, who shot or watched birds or
chased foxes. She hadn't met a single farm labourer either; as far as she
could recall, everyone she had met worked in offices and were managers

or directors. But they seemed to be keen on country life, even though half of them were new to it. And then, she said, there was George.

He came in at that point, limping badly, and we exchanged symptoms. I told him about my back, and he told me about his knee, which he had wrenched trying to kick a hen. He then started talking about the village. Now I have known George a long time, but not this George. In Lampeter they will be reading the pronouncements of a rural Savonarola.

The village was doomed, he said. Doomed. There was no village community. He turned to me. 'You're not on anything, are you? You don't mow the village green.' I said I had a bad back but George ignored me. 'You're not even on the parish council. What do you do for the village?'

'I go to the pub.' Then in a moment of inspiration, remembering Zorba the Greek ('I have fought for my country, I have raped for my country'), I said, 'I have drunk for this village.'

George swept this aside. The weekenders had come, he declared, who were death to a village. 'Weekend wooftahs,' muttered George. And where had the children gone? Of the hundred or so in the school, he doubted whether twenty children came from the village now. Young families just could not afford the houses. When his boys left school, he went on, there would be no way in which they could be part of the old life ever again. They would have to be forcibly pushed out of the nest.

I thought I would wish him luck in this, as his eldest is the size of a house, but on reflection kept that to myself. All this time the lady in the mauve suit was looking from one face to the other.

'Take the village bus,' said George. 'We have one a day. It leaves at 7.15 in the morning but goes to the centre of Northampton, where there are no factories. They're all on the outskirts now. That's why most mornings the bus is empty, and I should know, I'm up with the mail. This village is totally car-orientated.'

As for fresh air, it was the most unhealthy place he had ever known. The coughing queues in the post office. The grumbling. The danger of enquiring after anyone's health because of what might come out. 'Dreadful, dreadful. You know that nervous breakdown Elizabeth had? I've caught it now.' After twenty-four years he said he couldn't wait to be away.

'So where's the caravan stopping next?'

'Derbyshire,' said George. 'They've got some lovely stone houses up there. Villages are real in Derbyshire.'

The rural dream, when you are made to think about it, is always a little further. We could end up on the Solway Firth, George and I, and that chap in Lampeter.

1996

The Green Lane to Nowhere

ONCE UPON A TIME, not far from here, there was a Green Man; he wore a green felt hat that had belonged to his aunt, held feasts in which every course was green, and dispensed green jelly babies that a friendly Asian shopkeeper had laboriously picked out for him ('Can't imagine anyone else doing that'). But chiefly he loved a Green Lane.

The Green Man goes back a long way in folklore. Part horror, part reminder in a bleak time that the leaves will return, he appeared to Arthur at Camelot in the little dead days after Christmas. So it is appropriate we should remember him now, as, jaded by old films and cold turkey, we sit around bravely trying not to murder our relations.

But the Green Lane could be even older than he is. It runs from Northamptonshire to Banbury and was old when the Romans built Watling Street, for they cut across it. Today it takes every form an English thoroughfare can take, being in different places a metalled and numbered road, a lane and a bridle path. But for one two-mile stretch it looks as it has looked for thousands of years, sprawling, rutted, deep in mud, and you can imagine its pre-history when this was a quarter of a mile across.

It was always there, even on the oldest maps. Parish boundaries go up to it and it avoids villages, which would have been a great advantage to the drovers coming down it, trying to keep their herds together. It was the conjunction of the ancients when the Green Man came to the Green Lane.

His name was Lou Warwick and he was a local journalist when in 1981, alarmed at the overgrown state of those surviving two miles, he formed the Green Friends with a group of local ramblers. At first it was a pressure group. Its members included a bank manager, a railway clerk, a schoolteacher, a carpenter and men in local government, most of them in their sixties and all dedicated to getting farmers to take care of the Lane.

Which in time the farmers did, planting a screen of trees and even drain-
ing parts of it.

But that was just the beginning. Warwick's imagination took fire and
Warwick, as his old friend Reg Jones recalled, 'Had a very fertile imagination, also a typewriter.' The Green Friends became a secret society; it
acquired passwords and its own folklore, including rites of initiation
enacted at midnight. 'Some of us thought it was barmy, but we went along
with it because of Lou,' said Reg Jones. 'It was so good-natured, even if
things got madder and madder so there were 14-mile walks through the
night ending in a champagne breakfast at some pub. Pubs played a big part
in it. Our wives thought we'd all gone off our heads but they liked the fact
that it kept us quiet.'

Members found themselves in a world of ritual and hierarchy, each of
them being awarded a title. There were only about twenty of them, but the
titles, which included Deputy Chief Slasher, Lay Writer of the Ballads,
Chief Verderer and Dawn Patroller, suggested a membership of thousands. What made it even more bizarre was that dogs were admitted on
equal terms and had their own titles. Warwick bombarded members with
material (in green envelopes delivered at dawn), wrote songs (on green
paper) set to music, which he played on a trumpet, devised meals which
began with green blancmange and ended with pea soup, and made a sound
recording of every walk, almost every step, they took. Bemusedly they
entered the fantasies he had choreographed for them.

They walked at night and got wet through; they fell into ditches and had
strange conversations with policemen; they pressed cold mud into their
palms and shook hands in the dark. And of course they drank a great deal,
stumbling out of pubs for all-night walks. 'It got to the point where one
night Lou turned up in a blizzard,' said Reg Jones. 'He said, "Everyone's
jibbed. You won't let me down will you?" I looked out and I couldn't see
anything, so Lou walked on his own around the town and then went home.

'Another night, November 1988, we had been having a drink in the village and it was a dirty wet night when Lou suddenly announced he was
going to walk all the way back to Northampton, 15 or more miles away.
We were very worried, as he'd not been well and couldn't see much in

daylight, let alone at night. The next morning I got a call from a transport café and knew he was on his way. He staggered into Northampton in the early afternoon. His last walk was that Boxing Day. He was quite ill by then but he wanted to complete 500 miles for the year. He did it, came home, took to his bed and didn't get up again. He died in April.'

They meet once a year now, in May on the eve of his birthday, when they do a night walk partly in his memory and partly in memory of those days when, grand and baffled, they walked with the Green Man.

1991

The Calming

MY OLD FRIEND the historian George Freeston is writing in his Book of Blisworth. 'We are only two months into the Calming but the lorries have already broken up the cobbles,' records Mr Freeston, opening a new chapter. 'This morning I watched a workman setting cement back in the cracks. He was cross-legged like a Hindu and looked happy.'

A hundred years ago it was the Taming, when some sort of order was brought to the cattle towns of the American Midwest by men like Wild Bill Hickok and Wyatt Earp. Now it is the Calming, and this time it is the turn of the villages of Middle England, though the men responsible for it sit in offices and have no names.

Stand with me here, by this flattened rabbit, and look down the hill as the Towcester road approaches the village of Blisworth. It is obvious we are at some sort of frontier here, for on either side what appear to be gate pillars have been built, only there is no gate. But there is a frontier, as the mile-long tailback of traffic testifies. You leave commonsense behind as you pass through this and enter a world of fantasy and lunatic self-assurance created by the Northamptonshire Planning and Transportation Department but paid for by you. A large sign informs you that you are in the Blisworth Traffic Calming.

Huge pavements wide enough for a Paris boulevard have been built, narrowing the village streets, and grey lines, the meaning of which no one understands, have been painted between them and the road. Cobbles have been laid, reducing traffic in places to a one-way flow. Still, you can cope with these, though the tyres of twenty cars were blown in the first week alone as they collided with the new sharp curves. The lunacy comes when the old main road meets a country lane, for then right of way is given to the lane. Juggernauts hurtle down this and are never seen again, or execute agonised three-point turns as every junction becomes a place of terror and indecision. And it is worst for those who have lived here all their lives.

Meet Maureen Williams, caretaker of the village school ('site supervisor, if you please'), a lady whom no one in his right mind would cross, but one so demoralised by the Calming that she has not yet had the courage to drive out of a village where she has lived for thirty years – *in case she will not be able to get back.*

Meet George Freeston, a man entranced, saying quiet prayers to the Providence that has reserved this wonder for his old age. And meet Christopher Fiddes, international mural artist and beleaguered chairman of the parish council who reaped the whirlwind when he invited the county council to solve the traffic problems of Blisworth.

The village straddles the main Northampton to Oxford road, which means that since the days of stagecoaches, it has called for a by-pass. It got one three years ago, which was completed so quickly the council did not have the signposts ready. For a while a four-lane carriageway was a lost road going nowhere. Yet where *does* it go? Mr Freeston maintains that the by-pass goes to Sainsbury's, for it ends on the western outskirts of Northampton, and the young executives bursting out of the town centre continue to use the old A43. For is it not passing brave to accelerate an Audi Quattro through the streets of Blisworth? But look at them now, white-faced with anxiety and unable to get out of second gear, or brick-red as they rev in bitterness. They did not deserve this; nobody deserved this.

As in Greek myth, huge forces are at war, but in place of the warring gods there is the undeclared war between the Ministry of Transport ('roads, roads, ROADS') and the Department of the Environment. The county councils are in the vanguard of the Department's campaign against traffic, and Calming is their flavour of the month.

'Give it time, give it time,' pleads Christopher Fiddes, who hoped at most for a few ramps in the road and got this. 'I know it's contrary to commonsense, but Blake called commonsense, "the sense all idiots possess". Perhaps this is a Blakeian scheme.' To date, vandalisation of his car has cost him £520, as nastier elements showed dissent.

'I'm just waiting for a bang,' says Mrs Williams. 'Every night I hear the screech of tyres, and every morning I see skid marks. I hate it, I hate it. Whoever thought this up should be sacked at once.'

When Wheelie Bins came to Blisworth, the local district council mounted a PR campaign, showing residents how to lift the lids, but when the traffic scheme came, it materialised in their midst like the Tardis. The parish council is now in almost permanent session – and every morning the traffic jam is a few hundred yards longer.

'In this month the Calming came,' writes George Freeston in the Book of Blisworth, 'and the Uproar began.' Soon it will be your turn.

1993

The Invasion of the Wheelie Bins

O UR NEW BINS have just come. The public relations campaign had been so long, we had started to believe we were the victims of some elaborate fantasy. But then one morning last week we woke and there they were, like the Second Front. Inside each lid there was a set of ten instructions. The first of these read, in letters overlaid for emphasis: 'On the day of collection place your container at the kerbside with the handles facing the road.'

Now you might think we are just talking about something you fill with rubbish and, on an appointed day, place in front of your house. Not so. To the South Northants District Council a bin is as complex as a Stinger rocket launcher. The mujahedin fighting the Russians in the mountains of Afghanistan have taken delivery of Stingers with far less instruction. For through our letterboxes have come engineering diagrams, dotted lines showing the angle of the opening lid and the degree of tip necessary to move the bin on its two back wheels. We have been given a hotline number to ring at the council offices (though the three times I tried it there was no answer). Demonstration teams have toured the villages.

The bins are provided free, are three times the size of the old ones and have wheels under them. Made in Germany, they cost £27 each and to the council are clearly the most important thing since Domesday. The poll tax remains as mysterious as the Black Death, our MEP may be as remote as King Arthur – but when it came to the Wheelies the council embarked on a policy of public instruction unique in local government.

Leaflets spoke movingly of the hardships of bin men under the old dispensation and of rubbish blowing through the streets. Nothing was left to chance as the New Order (which has already come to a quarter of all British local authorities) was spelt out.

And in case we still did not appreciate this, 'Residents will be able to see the new containers and discuss the benefits . . . at the following locations.'

A special trailer was towed through the villages, with a representative from the German firm, a man from the council and a young woman making notes. The trailer stopped, an awning was drawn out and the bins produced. Domesday itself must have been something like this – another small group of travellers, perhaps another awning, and then the villagers crowding worriedly around the strangers.

For this was the wonderful thing. By going to these lengths the council managed not to enlighten but to worry people. They, too, had begun to suspect something enormous was about to happen to them. 'Yes,' said a lady peering into a bin, 'it IS big enough to take a body.' Everyone stared at her and one old man said vaguely that it was the thin end of the wedge.

The young man from the German company wore dark glasses and was clearly at the end of his public relations tether. Asked whether it would be possible to break the bin, he said in a dead voice that it was possible to break anything if you were determined enough. The man from the council talked about the eight irreconcilables in 14,000 who had announced they were having nothing to do with Wheelies. Some people, he said with emphasis, just did not like bins.

People worried about gradients, cattle grids, about collection on bank holidays (though there had never been any before). And then, out of nowhere, there was a sudden, bitter row. A lady active in parish affairs asked what redress they would have against the Wheelies. None, she was told, except the democratic one of the right to vote out the council. That did it.

An unsmiling pale young man, St Just in his beginnings, said the bins had been foisted on them, which in a way they had, being free. The old man said again it was the thin end of the wedge, but this time less vaguely. My friend George and I walked away, quite baffled.

George has a plaque on his wall to show the village was in the Domesday Book. He is thinking of adding a second: '*Today the wheelie bins came upon us.*'

1989

PART TWELVE

Exits

My Neighbour

S HE DIED WHEN I was away and I missed the funeral. I owed her much; she was my first introduction to institutionalised old age, and this could not have been more complete. In her last three years, between the age of eighty-six and eighty-nine, she was in four hospitals, a local authority home and four private nursing homes, being expelled from three of them. She was, it was said, difficult, an adjective almost entirely reserved for the old now.

When I was small my grandfather lived with us. He sat in a chair, as the old had always done, and the family swirled about him. But this lady, at the end of a busy life, ricocheted around the Welfare State like a bearing in a pinball game.

Yet just five years ago she was our neighbour, burning garden rubbish, talking of her years in the Post Office and of the time she had her own car ('I went everywhere then'). Poor thing, her travels had not even begun. She was tough, independent, sharp-tongued. When I remarked after a lavish local wedding that the English made a lot of fuss over getting married, she gave me one of her alarming grins. 'The Welsh keep that for funerals,' she said.

When we went to see her, my daughter, aged two, would steal her stick – but all she ever said was, 'Leave her, she's young.' Unmarried, she loved children, the naughtier the better. By then she had moved to an old folks' bungalow, and it was the start of her decline. Suddenly she could not find things, so a visit would be given over to a search for her teeth. She became dependent on a kindly next-door neighbour and it was when this lady was on holiday that the travels began. Complaining of stomach pains she was put in hospital, fell out of bed and broke her wrist. In a world which was full of new faces she began to forget.

There was an old folks' home – the old, immaculately clean, sitting silently around the walls as though awaiting dance partners who never came. The television was on all day. Everywhere we went to see her the television was on all day. She broke a leg and there was another hospital. By now, as far as she was concerned, she could have been on a base on the Moon, and when I talked brightly about the weather outside, her sharp eyes stared through me. I saw my first Reality Orientation chart on the wall there, inviting the old to identify the day, the month and the names of their children.

Sometimes I would pass the locked bungalow in the village and think of the photographs inside of her brother and of the niece who had died, aged four; little indices to a life which had slipped its moorings.

There were days when she did not know me but at other times the old devilment flashed briefly. I asked whether the vicar had been to see her. 'Vicars? I'm beyond vicars, boy.' No doubt she was difficult. I was told so often enough. She refused to walk on her healing legs; she was old and she was cross at being old, so there must have been many case conferences off-stage. We visited her in 1930s villas, in glum hospitals with whole wards empty. 'Do you know where my bed is here?' she asked.

For months she was in that last wastepaper basket of the Social Services, a Victorian mental hospital the size of a town, listening expressionlessly as a neighbour talked of her close friendship with Mrs Thatcher.

At the end she seemed content. In an Edwardian country house the nurses had accepted her as a character and, talking to one, she suddenly fell asleep; her travels were over.

They buried her on her birthday.

1987

The Parish Clerk

FIRST THE KETTLE DRUMS and then the groaning of horns as, after thirty-eight years in a job he once said had much in common with the Grand Mastership of the Knights Templar, a great man retires. The banner of the Order is at half-mast as Parish Clerk Weekley winds slowly out of history. And with him goes someone who has tolerantly endured my fantasies, a sturdy ex-schoolmaster, a mountain-climbing, *Guardian*-reading man, his eyebrows borrowed from a car wash, the real Parish Clerk Weekley. But watch him, too, for this was a man whose responsibilities were greater than any I conjured up. For thirty-eight years he tended the seed plot of democracy.

Parish councils were established 102 years ago as the unit of British government, and this is where it all starts, Parliament, monarch and all. At the very first meeting the first Parish Secretary of this village was solemnly given permission 'to buy the necessary stationery, also lamp oil', and there was an air of the frontier about the proceedings as they debated their first priority – a water supply for the village. Three years they debated it until the last squire, forced to sit through it all, intervened to say he would pay. He then paid for a new church clock, a pavement and a new set of instruments for the village band. A century ago the parish clerk spent most of his time proposing votes of thanks in a brave new world.

His name was John Franklin and he served fifty-seven years. Then there were the troubled 1950s, clerks coming and going like kings in the Wars of the Roses, before John Weekley took over in 1958 and the great debates of democracy were resumed . . .

'Dog mess,' said the Clerk. 'Whenever a parish council meets anywhere in England it always ends up discussing the threat of dog mess.' Oh, the summer evenings I have walked the streets with him, our hands in plastic bags, hoping the threat would not still be warm.

With him I have walked the footpaths, agonised over the vandalism in the cricket pavilion, and gloried in the village's one great success story, its cemetery. Every year the cemetery shows a profit and every year in his report the parish clerk shows due gratitude to the dead. But then the dead would not let him be. Like most of the village, they may not have turned up for parish meetings, but they had left their instructions. A medieval haberdasher frantically ironing out his soul at the end, a seven-teenth-century Duchess, they had left him £3,000 a year in charities to administer. 'The poor are a problem,' he told me once. 'It requires such delicacy to select them now.'

It was not always so. *The poor will long remember / The kind repast they did enjoy / On the 24th of September.* Widows were also easy once, for they had to wear the initials of the Duchess's daughter on their chest. No initials, no charity.

'But we had a woman apply once. This chap pointed out she couldn't be a widow as she'd never married. But we overruled him.'

We never had the drama of the Northants village that left a field from which the rent provided the poor with six sacks of coal a year, then sold the field to a millionaire developer. That village has a cricket pitch now of county standard, and if the old deign to visit the nearest town, they are fer-ried there in chauffeur-driven cars.

The only drama we had was when a developer applied for planning permission for a road to a close of houses he had built. It was only when they sleepily examined the map that they saw the road had no end but streamed on, relentless as the M1, into the fields. 'We saw him off,' said Parish Clerk Weekley.

His predecessor looked for water like Moses, but Weekley at the end found himself smothering in questionnaires, as a distant bureaucracy, like the dead, would not let him be. Did we still have a shop? Did we like the police? Were there teenagers? Now, like the Emperor Diocletian retired among his cabbages, he does not have to answer any of them. *Ave atque vale.*

1998

The Colonel's Wife

A DUCK SITS ON a windowsill. Made of modern Venetian glass, it has one green wing and one blue and is not a thing of beauty. But once not even the Holy of Holies was so forbidden. Had you picked it up, had you moved it just a few inches, the whole small world would have trembled. At five, my daughter, watching from a distance, believed Saddam Hussein had gone to war to get his hands on something you can now toss from hand to hand, and nobody will care. The autocrat of the bungalow, sinking in the spirals of Alzheimer's disease, has been three weeks in a residential home and has forgotten there ever was a duck, with one wing green, the other blue. This is how a life comes to an end in England now.

Her daughters had never discussed the possibility of a home with her; she was too far gone for that. But then they had never discussed anything, for she disliked intimacy. Mostly she talked, bright cocktail party chatter, as if they had just met, telling them anecdotes they had heard many times, although they did not remind her. When she had a small stroke, a sherry glass falling from her hand, her speech slurring into silence, the two of them who saw this, though by then middle-aged, felt unable afterwards to tell her what had happened.

So in the end, saying they were taking her out to lunch, they drove her to the home and left her, just as forty years earlier she had left them at their boarding schools. They waved goodbye gaily, only this time the bewildered young faces staring down the drive had been replaced by a bewildered old one.

I first met her and her late husband in retirement twenty years ago. His record was impressive: a full colonel in his thirties, subsequently a colonial administrator, but it was not his kingdom you entered when you came to

244

their house. The first thing I noticed was the labelling of jars, not just the marmalades and the years they were made; this woman labelled everything, even jars of pickles with the manufacturer's name already on them. On the other side, in her handwriting, was 'pickles'. I had never encountered this wish to control before.

It could only happen in an upper-middle class English family: elsewhere her dominance would have been challenged by constant rows or imposed by direct commands. Here there were no commands, for nothing was said directly. But if she said, 'Oh dear, I seem to have left my spectacles upstairs,' an elderly gentleman leapt to his feet. He had been schooled to authority by prefects, the Army, his superiors, and now in retirement, as he dwindled, there was an ultimate authority which had once been blunted by social life, by parties and menus, the bossing of servants, the judging at dog shows (like all such women, she loved dogs). And now there was nothing to blunt it.

Had there been a job, her energy and her will would have been funnelled, but it was her tragedy, even more that of her family, that all she ever became was someone's wife. Only once did she ever admit to her power, when she showed me the alcove, which was the size of a bathroom, off her bedroom, which was where her clothes hung. Her husband, she said, had a little cupboard at the end of the passage, and for a moment there was a grin, so devilish and gone so quickly that I had to remind myself it had been there.

Her husband would have been puzzled had you asked him about the roaring ego he had partly assembled. He wore the clothes she chose, went on the holidays she demanded, and at the end slipped away, dying in his sleep. It was the one rebellious act of his life. On his grave, without irony, an emotion she never knew, she had this cut: 'Be still, and know that I am God.'

And then the quiet came, and the confusion with it, when she forgot names and, as resident carers came and went, thought herself in a hotel. They took away her keys, locked her front gate, and after the last dog died, three weeks ago, she entered the home. I have been to see her there, among the judges' widows and the retired chief constables, all sitting round the walls. Each private room bristles with photographs most of them have forgotten.

Just as she has forgotten the duck with one wing green, the other blue, I have just carefully put back in its old place.

1997

A Memory as Old as the Century

OUR OLDEST INHABITANT leaves the village tomorrow. He is ninety-three years old and it will be the first time, apart from during the Great War, he has been away. With his usual neatness he has arranged his photographs of streets, school and church, adding some of his old garden so his memories can be indexed in the residential home 40 miles away.

He is full of enthusiasm, being tired, he tells me, of cooking for himself. Also, slowly over the last few years, he has begun to appreciate how very old he is. Recently he had a photograph printed in the local newspaper, taken in 1931, when he and some colleagues from the motor trade went on a day's outing to Fort Dunlop. He hoped it would prompt some response, and there was none. 'That's when it dawned on me, they were all dead.' Four years ago he went to a reunion of Royal Air Force mechanics at which everyone was given a number referring to his year of entry – but his own was so much earlier, nobody had thought to include it. Those who turned up in 1989 at RAF Halton were startled to see a small gentleman ambling round with a badge with a large zero attached to his lapel.

He was born here in a farmhouse in the fields, now in ruins. He courted his wife in the house where I now live; she lies in the churchyard I can see from my window. He opened the first village garage and wrote the first village history, of which he is part, for in the old school records his name recurs. Across eighty years he has kept his exercise books, all in immaculate copperplate, even a rare mis-spelling. Manoeuvres. Manoeuvres. Manoeuvres. Each one was written out ten times, for this was when teachers cared about such things.

In the spring of 1914 Europe was a parade ground but the Oldest Inhabitant was writing, over and over, 'Representative Government.

Representative Government. Representative Government.' But then there were no more worries about Representative Government, for it was September 1914. 'The Austrians have been badly beaten by the Serbs and the Russians are on their way to Berlin. The Germans are in full retreat.' He was fourteen and believed what he read in the papers.

There was more of this, with a song about General John French also on the road to Berlin, that presumably crowded thoroughfare. He copied out a hair-raising poem, in full, called 'Fall In' by Harold Begbie, about girls who would ignore men who hadn't enlisted – all part of the pressure exerted on the young in village schools.

But, in the midst of it, one young man was planning his future with the care of a moon shot. There would be an apprenticeship in the motor trade first, he wrote in an essay, then a small shop, a bigger shop, a garage. And that was how things turned out. 'If I got plenty of money,' he wrote, 'and got too old to do much business, I should get a large house in the country and keep a motor and several horses and a carriage . . .'

The Oldest Inhabitant, as he now is, must have been struck by his own *foile de grandeur* for he added, in parenthesis, 'Or get a little cottage and have the old age pension and go about on a tricycle.' It was not meant as humour, for this was a very serious young man. Yet the irony is that in his later years, when he began to find walking difficult, the Oldest Inhabitant did just this, buying himself an electric carriage on three wheels in which he trundled from his bungalow to the shops.

He has seen so much go in his time, that whole world of horses and blacksmiths, and a village in which everyone worked on the land or was in service ('only I branched out'). He has known ten vicars and almost as many schoolmasters. The village railway station has gone and also the Methodist chapel ('which I then desecrated by turning it into a car show-room'). Even the strange old squire has gone: 'Funny mousy little man with a shifty look', who used to address the small boys on the duties of being a good citizen ('which he never was'). But the Oldest Inhabitant will not be drawn on the squire's little weakness, though once, badgered by me, he totted up a whole cricket team of his bastards. None of this went into his village history.

The greatest change in his long life has been the coming of strangers, for with the car came commuting, and with commuting a whole society of villagers no one sees, who are gone with the morning and return at night. The Oldest Inhabitant is leaving a village where people no longer know him, though, as he acknowledged, the irony is that, in his business as a motor trader, he has been responsible for this.

His name is Philip Kingston, and he can now spell Representative Government.

1993

A House Clearance

PHOTOGRAPHS, BOXES full of them, suitcases, laundry chests; there were more than in some picture libraries, photographs of deserted tropical beaches, guards of honour, of large wild animals staring into the camera. It was ironic that it should be this of all weeks, with newspapers chorusing about the end of Empire, that we cleared the house of someone whose life had been part of that Empire. Everything had been packed and unpacked so many times, taken in and out of store, assembled and reassembled. Tea chests and lists, lists and tea chests, for this was a woman for whom packing had been an art form. A memsahib lived here, in a long gardening epilogue to Empire in an English village.

That epilogue is over, but not the life. She lives in the moment now, like a very small child, singing carols on summer afternoons with the other old ladies in the home.

Sarawak and its People; *Malay for Mems*. Then the whims of his masters sent her husband westward, and there were boxes of seashells and feathers and old calypso records. East again, to an Africa that had the Wind of Change blowing through it, and he, straddling the old world and the new, found himself the first Chief Justice of an independent African state.

So it was that I came upon a moment of history, finding letters marked: 'Personal and Secret', which recorded the first confrontation between the judge and his new President. Members of the President's party had taken to bullying their defeated political opponents, and the Chief Justice was incredulous. 'It is as though after a Cup Final the victors are gathering around the dressing-room of their opponents, uttering all sorts of abuse and threats.'

But the President, for there was a real friendship between the two, was conciliatory. 'Our task is not made easier for us when these chaps refuse to respect the National Flag and the National Anthem . . .' Delicately, he touched on tribalism in what was then a brand new democratic state.

What was I to do with fifty years of letters? Horribly cheerful ones dispatched to small girls in English boarding schools; letters to his mother from a man wrestling with his religious conscience in a world war; letters dutiful, some mind-numbingly boring. There would have been people like me, sitting in a heap of parchments at the end of the Roman Empire, the packhorses moving impatiently outside. If only they had kept some of them. So, crossly, I opened another file for a moment of post-colonial history that may one day interest some man in a library.

All round me was chaos as we dismantled the life laid out here, its taste in books, records, furniture, the wedding dress in cream and gold which has lain in a Chinese trunk for sixty years, the silver cup recording that she won the 440, the hurdles, the long jump, in one unimaginable golden day.

This is something nobody writes about, the closing of a house. They write about its purchase, whole magazines are devoted to its interior decoration, but nobody writes about what each one of us has to do once, perhaps twice, in our lives. The British Telecom letter addressed to the next owner awaited his coming in the hall, and it was that twilight between the estate agents and the clearance men. Through it her daughters moved, in middle age meeting their mother for the first time in these collections, in these chests they had not been allowed to open until now.

I found a photograph of her aged two, a stout girl staring, and it was the face of someone determined to have her own way whatever the cost. Later she learned to smile in photographs. Me on safari. Me with the chief of police. Me skiing. Her small children appeared from time to time like studio props, but then, their travels over, this couple who had been everywhere, photographed everything, just photographed their flowers. I threw away eighty pictures of roses.

She threw nothing away. Envelopes were marked 'desk keys', 'suitcase keys', 'clock keys', although none of these fitted any desk, suitcase or clock which we had assembled in the middle of the floor. But one key fitted. We locked the door for the last time, pushed the keys through the letterbox, and it was an end.

1998

ENDINGS

IN THE PUB THE OTHER NIGHT I met a man whose father had just died. I sympathised the way you do when you don't know someone well, and expected an equally formal reply. But this, when it came, wasn't formal at all. What he had found distressing, he said bitterly, was that so few people had called on his mother to offer their condolences. He had expected them to in a village.

And he began to tell me something of his father, how at one time he had been a schoolmaster among the Sioux in the Black Hills of Dakota. Now this was an old gentleman I had nodded to in passing for years, yet I knew nothing of this. Had I stopped just once, I should have met a fascinating man. But I hadn't stopped.

When people talk about the country, they have precise ideas about what they expect to find. They see a pub where men stand the oldest inhabitant drinks, where a man knows his neighbours and in times of distress will call to offer his condolences. But it isn't like that. There was an oldest inhabitant in the pub when I first came to the village and, yes, men did stand him drinks. Only one night they stood him so many he fell over, after which he was so embarrassed he never came to the pub again. I doubt whether one in ten of us could even name the oldest inhabitant now. When that happens, the conduit to a community's past is blocked and the process initiated by which, relentlessly, this stops being a community at all. Who planted the trees on the village green? Whose coat of arms hangs outside the pub? Soon such things will be as puzzling to us as the features of a station concourse.

People mention their children when they talk about moving to the country. They see them walking to school across the village green. And, yes, there is a village green and there is a school, but most children come by car or bus. Few walk because the rural dream has lifted the cost of most houses out of the reach of first-time buyers. It is the safety and the certainty of forty years ago that people hope to buy into when they move. Yet, from this term on, the school doors are to be locked during lessons and fitted with an entryphone, a development I found as much of a shock as that felt across Europe in the third century when the Emperor Aurelian found it necessary to build the first wall around Rome. Yet people still come here, and the reason why we don't call to offer condolences is that we, being refugees, don't know each other.

We are not fleeing wars, we are fleeing cities and change, but the result is similar. Professionally, we have nothing in common. Forty years ago we would have talked about the land, but the cars begin to leave before dawn and by nine o'clock I am one of perhaps half-a-dozen males below pensionable age left in the village. A man doing market research on booze once fell on me with whoops of joy, as though he had hooked a fish he thought extinct.

Who are we? In my time there have been a 'flavourologist', a secretary of a pop group's fan club, a former county cricketer, a lady who could work out how the long-dead looked from their skeletons, a man on the *Burlington Magazine*, someone who comes up with computer programmes that allow his employer to sack people by the town-load (he, of course, works from home), a sea captain. This village was old when William the Conqueror's tax assessors called, but it has never seen anything like us. Take the sea captain. He worked in shipping in London but chose to live as far from the sea as it was possible for a man to live on this island. Each night, around seven, he called into the pub on his way home. To him this was a sort of decompression chamber, where each night he drank two pints of beer, no more, no less, preferring to stand alone, not talking, as he made this re-entry.

Possibly he would have liked to hear chaps in corduroys talking about the crops, except they don't have the time. They are at the wheels of machinery so big and blazing with so many lights that these look like oil rigs lurching through the village day and night. Each year these machines are bigger, and, being unsprung, they crash over manhole covers in the small hours, jerking awake the quiet adulterers in the pub. Thus the harvest that nobody wants is gathered in.

Yet time passes and we are still here. Perhaps like the people in Rick's Bar in *Casablanca*, we no longer have anywhere else to go. But it is sad to be reminded, as I have just been reminded, that by our coming we brought the change we thought to escape. Play it again, Sam.

Last November I was burning leaves when a new neighbour stuck his head over the fence. ''Scuse me, but can't you take those to the tip like every-one else?' It was the ''Scuse me' that did it: as soon as I heard those reproachful syllables, I knew the outriders of urban life had come.

It was like that morning in the seventh century when the Welsh saint Beuno, walking by the Severn, heard a man call to his dogs on the other bank: he was calling in English. The saint promptly decamped for the West, as I shall do, fleeing the barbecue and the glottal stop, for where I live, 80 miles north of London, it is not a matter of where the country begins, it is where London allows it to begin. The advance, like that of the early English, is inexorable.

So is its speed. Just after the War it was possible for Enoch Powell, in full hunting pink, to catch the Central Line of the London Underground and go fox-hunting. You knew where the country started then. Now London, like General MacArthur in his advance on Japanese-held islands in the Pacific, has vaulted on. Pockets of a tolerated country survive, of riding stables and immaculately gated tax-dodge farming, the world of Surrey and Buckinghamshire, and there are still enough fields in Essex for the East End gangs to bury their victims. But where does the mud start?

I used to think it started here. You leave Oxfordshire behind, with its white window-framed village houses called the Old Post Office, the Old School, the Old Chapel (though never the Old Slaughterhouse), and you enter a working county, a lovely, dirty, forgotten county, around which two motorways go. At least you did when I first moved here twenty-two years ago. But in that time I have seen two London hairdressers, with their pot-bellied Vietnamese pig, come and go, and a newcomer take legal action to stop a farmer driving his cows through the village. But of seven families farming before the War, three are still here. The frontier holds, but only just.

I find myself brooding over a photograph taken from the air. Such things are popular, and Parish Clerk Weekley has one which shows him sitting on his own roof, only they get taken from 100 feet up. The one I have is a little different: it was taken from 60 miles up, from a satellite. A town like Towcester is the size of the nail on my little finger, the M1 is a hairline fracture, and the only piece of geometry anywhere is the remorseless straight line, seen from space, of the old Roman Watling Street. The scale is 1–75,000, the photograph is 20 inches by 16 inches, its detail amazing.

I can see fields and reservoirs and a motorway service station, and, given the proper magnification, I could probably make out Parish Clerk Weekley still on his roof waiting for his next photocall. Until I was given this, I had not realised it was possible for members of the public to get their hands on such things. A print costs £60, which presumably restricts their popularity, as no farmer is going to want one when his yard is the size of a blackhead. Yet members of the public are beginning to buy these pictures, perhaps for peace of mind. For this is the earth as no bird has ever seen it, and you look down on a couple of hundred thousand people, their bodies invisible as microbes, and you are as distant from their worries and their rows as an angel. Look, you can just make out their by-passes and their parks, their racecourses and their research establishments, but at this height the street plans of their towns look like writhing maggots, a puff of cloud conceals an entire farm.

This was Middle England.

2002

DATE DUE		
MAY 2 2 2003		
JUN 1 4 2003		
JUN 2 4 2003		
JUL 1 7 2003		
OCT 2 4 2003		
DEC 1 1 2003		

5/03

Rogers, Byron

The green lane to nowhere